THE SQUIRREL MOTHER

stories

Megan Kelso

Fantagraphics Books
Seattle, Washington

Fantagraphics Books, Inc.
7563 Lake City Way
Seattle, WA 98115

Edited by Gary Groth
Designed by Tom Devlin
Promotion by Eric Reynolds
Published by Gary Groth & Kim Thompson

To receive a free catalogue of fine comics and books, call 1-800-657-1100 or visit our website at Fantagraphics.com.

Distributed in the U.S. by W.W. Norton and Company, Inc. (1-212-354-5500)
Distributed in Canada by Raincoast Books (1-800-663-5714)
Distributed in the UK by Turnaround Distribution (1-208-829-3009)

ISBN-13: 9-781-56097-746-9
ISBN-10: 1-56097-746-9
Printed in China

for msb
with love

CONTENTS

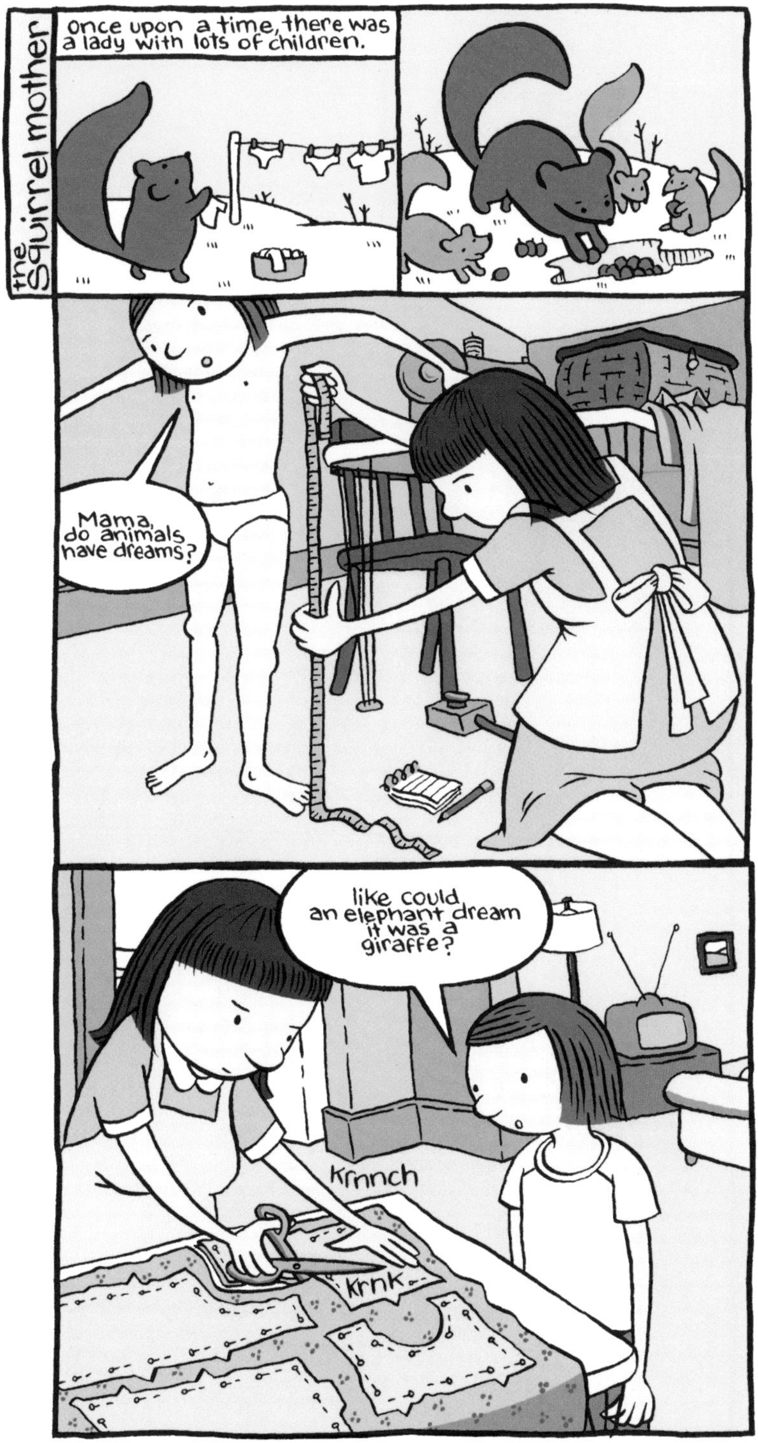
the Squirrel mother
Once upon a time, there was a lady with lots of children.
Mama, do animals have dreams?
like could an elephant dream it was a giraffe?
krnnch
krnk

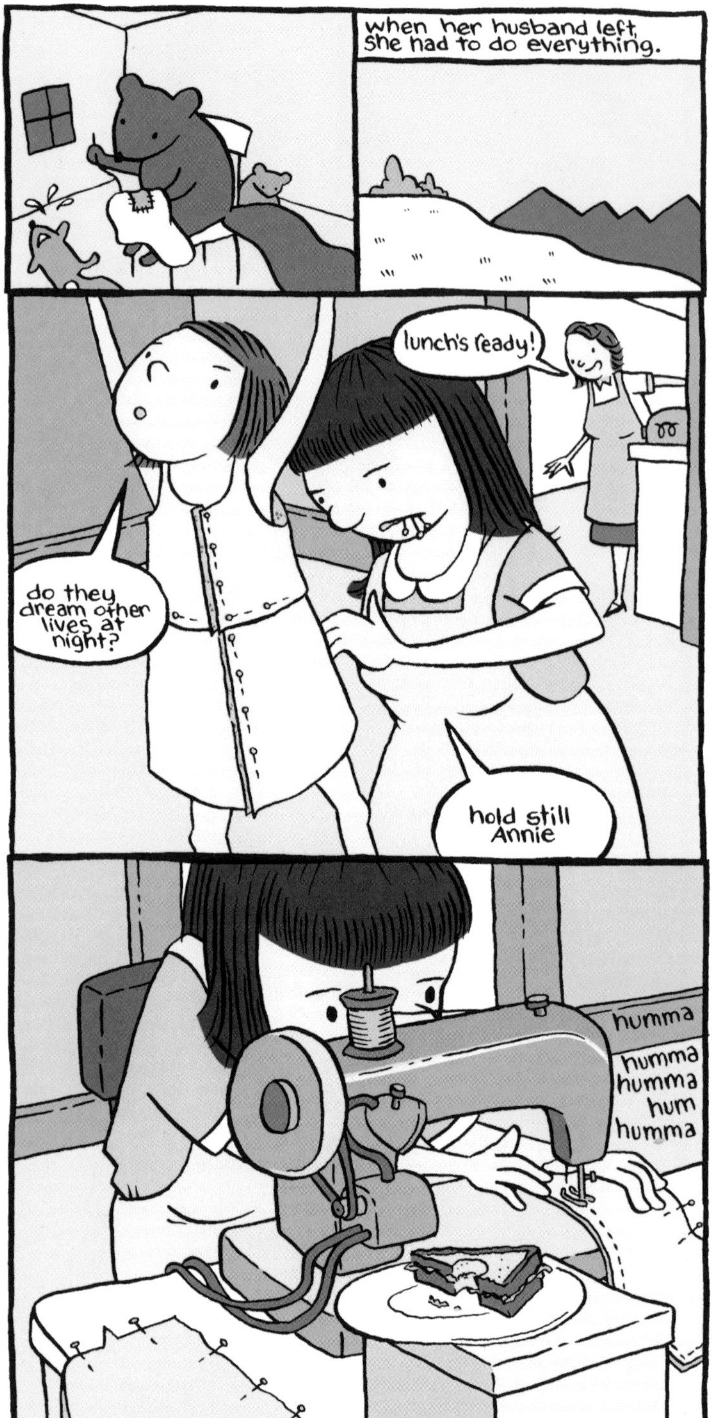
when her husband left, she had to do everything.
lunch's ready!
do they dream other lives at night?
hold still Annie
humma
humma
humma
hum
humma

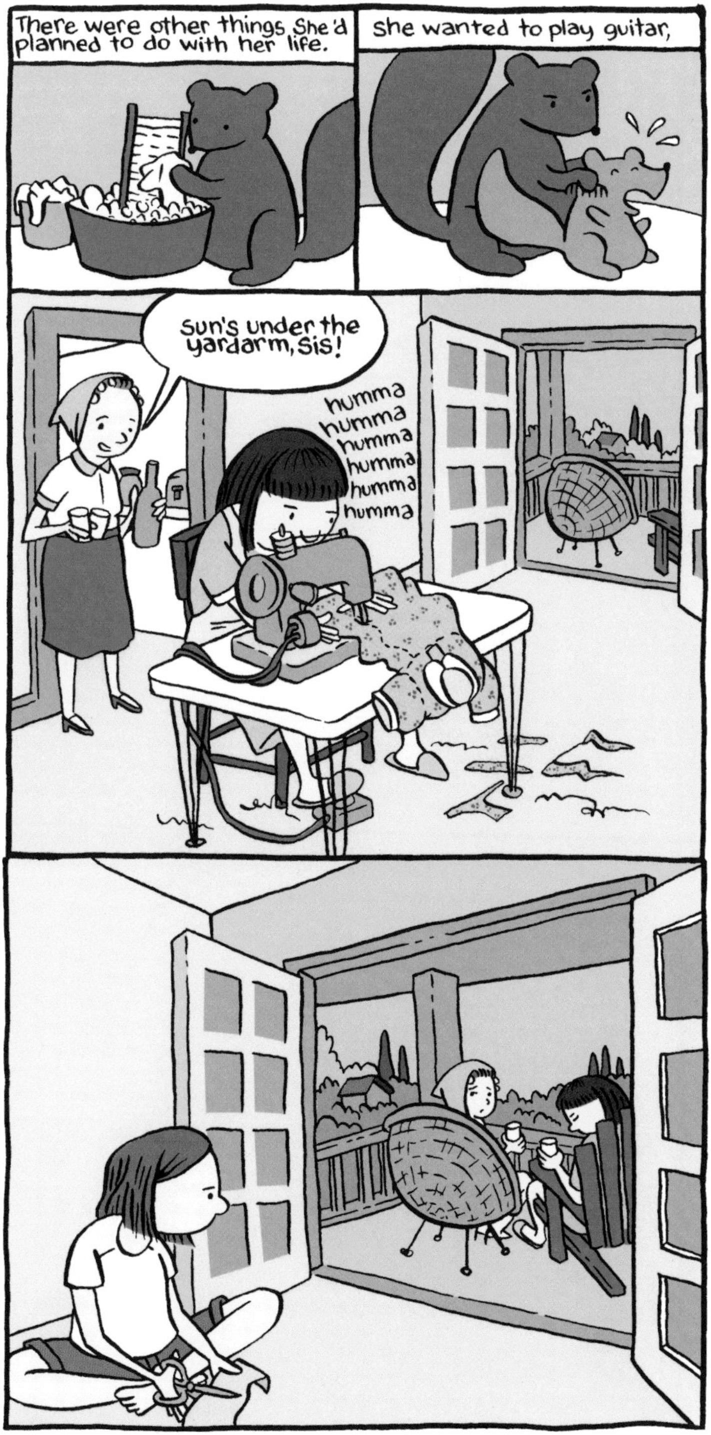
There were other things she'd planned to do with her life.
she wanted to play guitar,
Sun's under the yardarm, sis!
humma humma humma humma humma humma

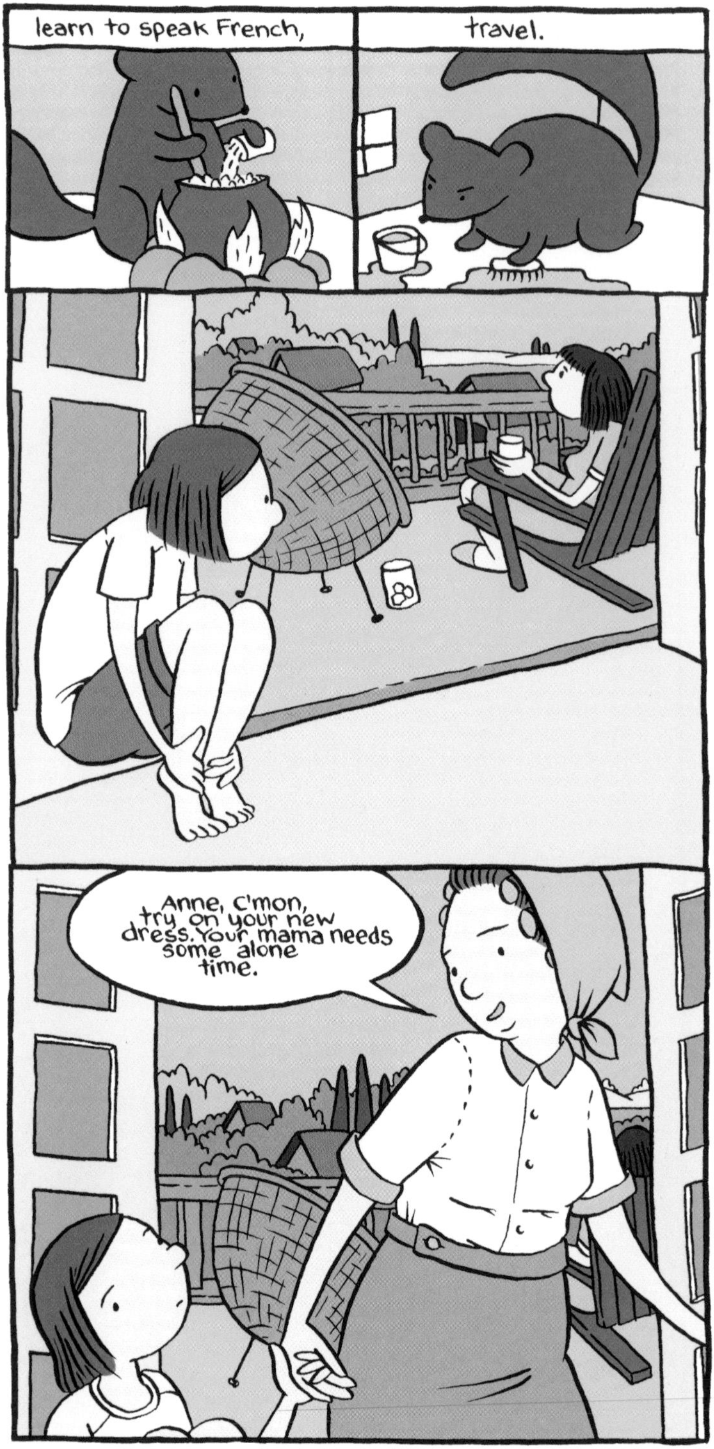
learn to speak French,
travel.
Anne, C'mon, try on your new dress. Your mama needs some alone time.

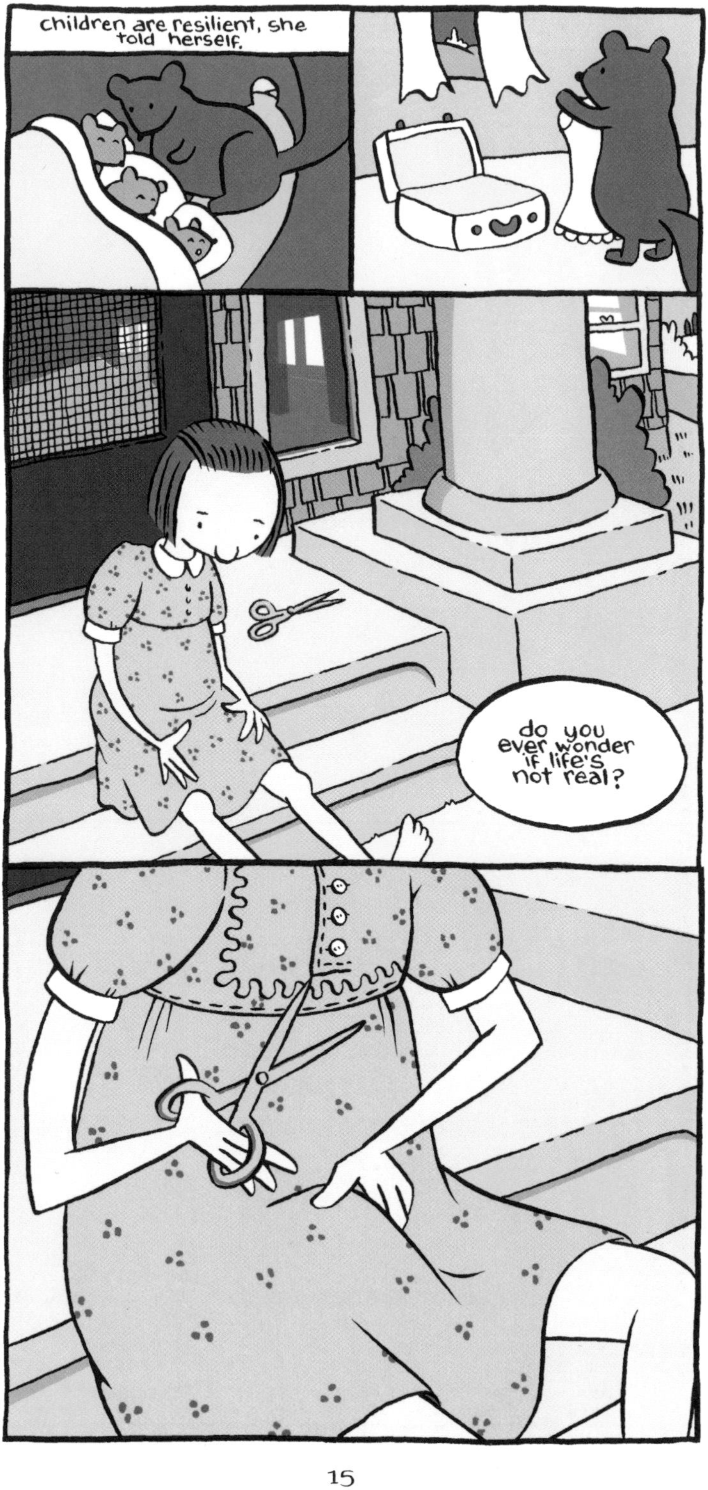
children are resilient, she told herself.
do you ever wonder if life's not real?

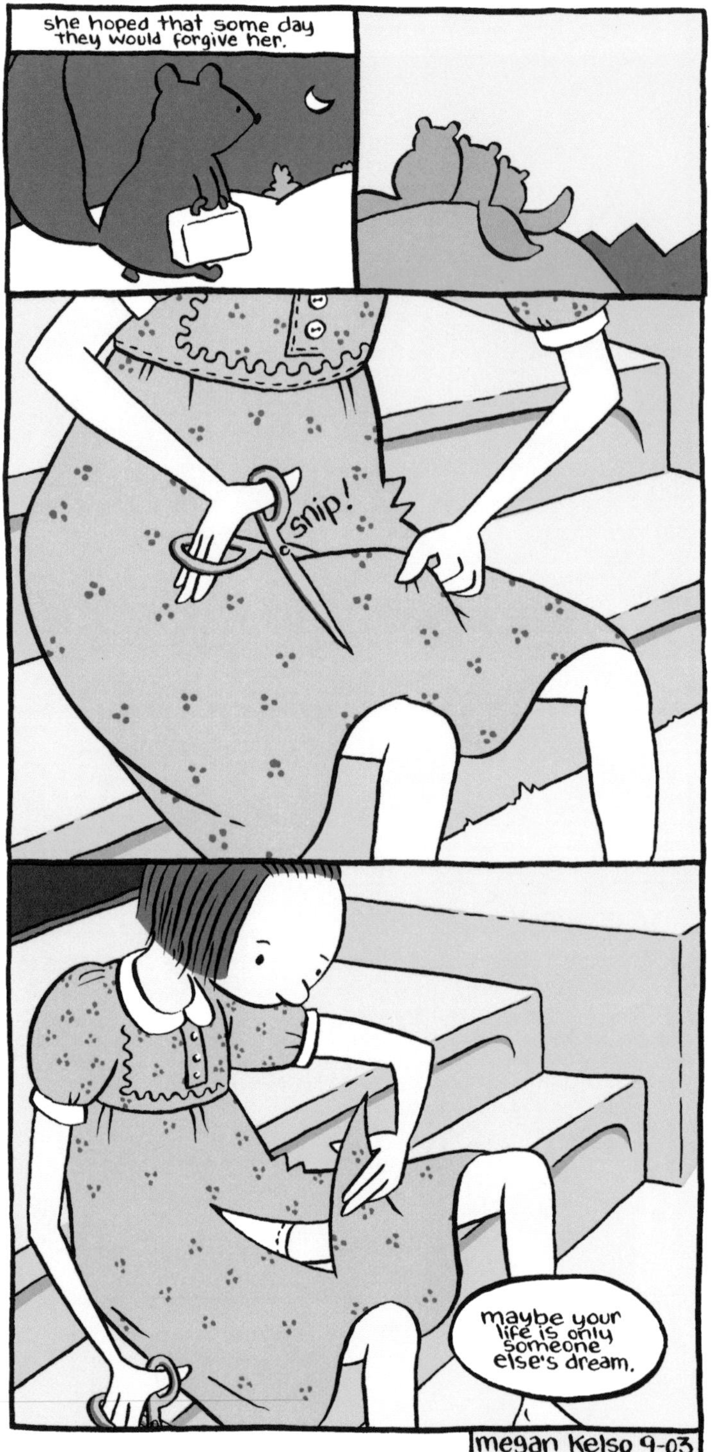
she hoped that some day they would forgive her.
snip!
maybe your life is only someone else's dream.
megan kelso 9-03

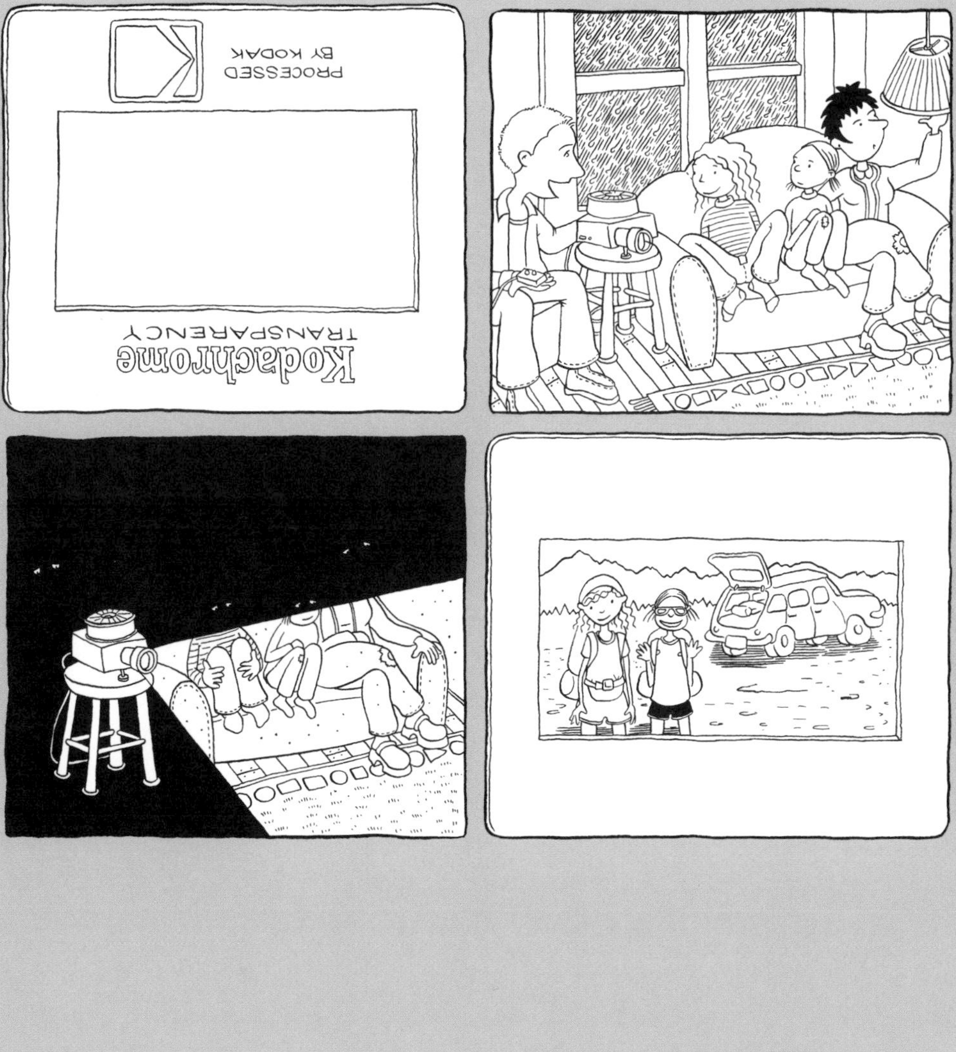
PROCESSED BY KODAK
Kodachrome TRANSPARENCY

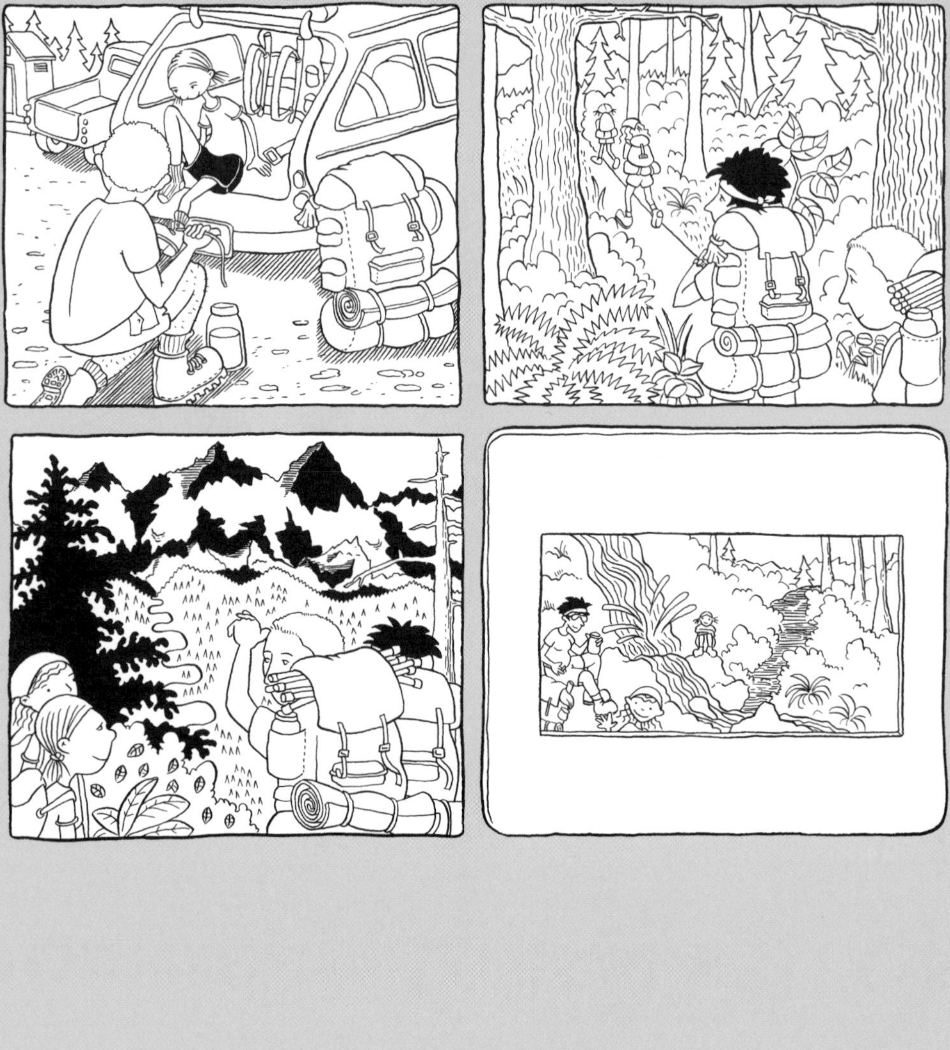

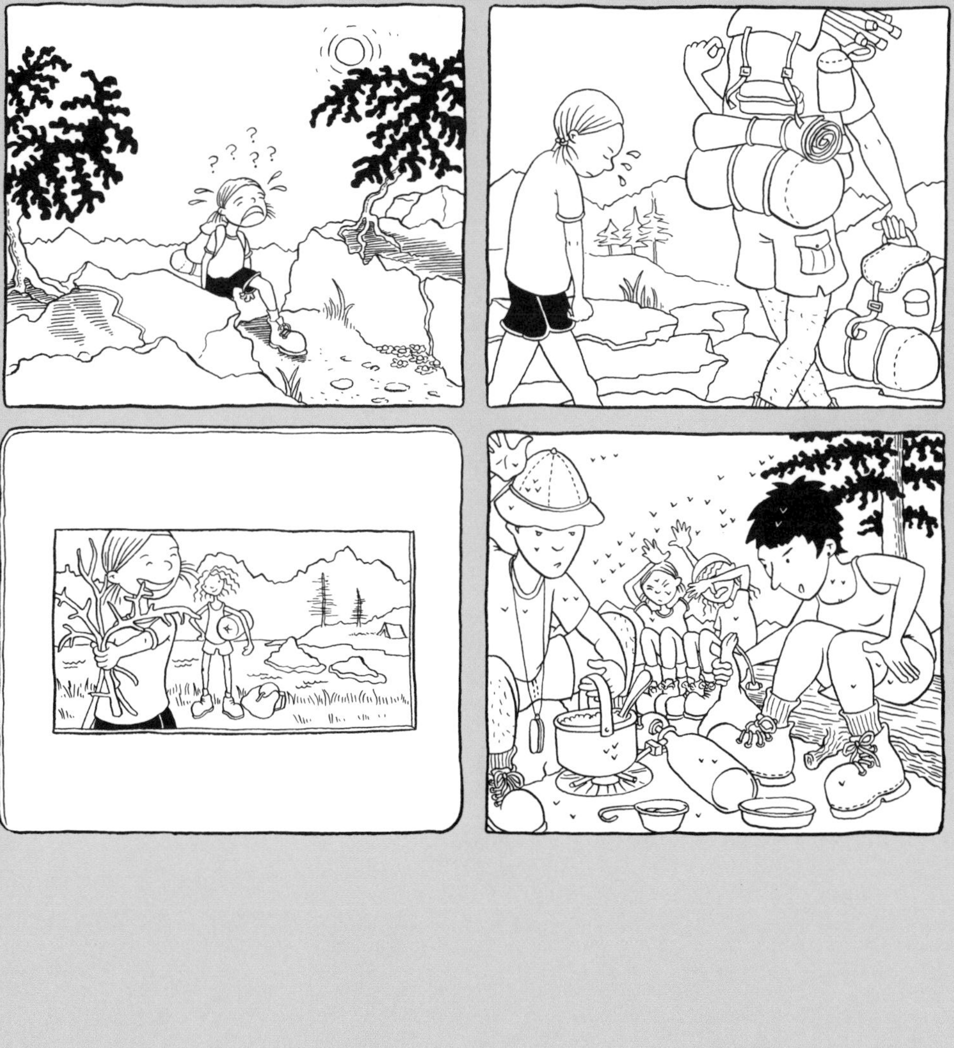

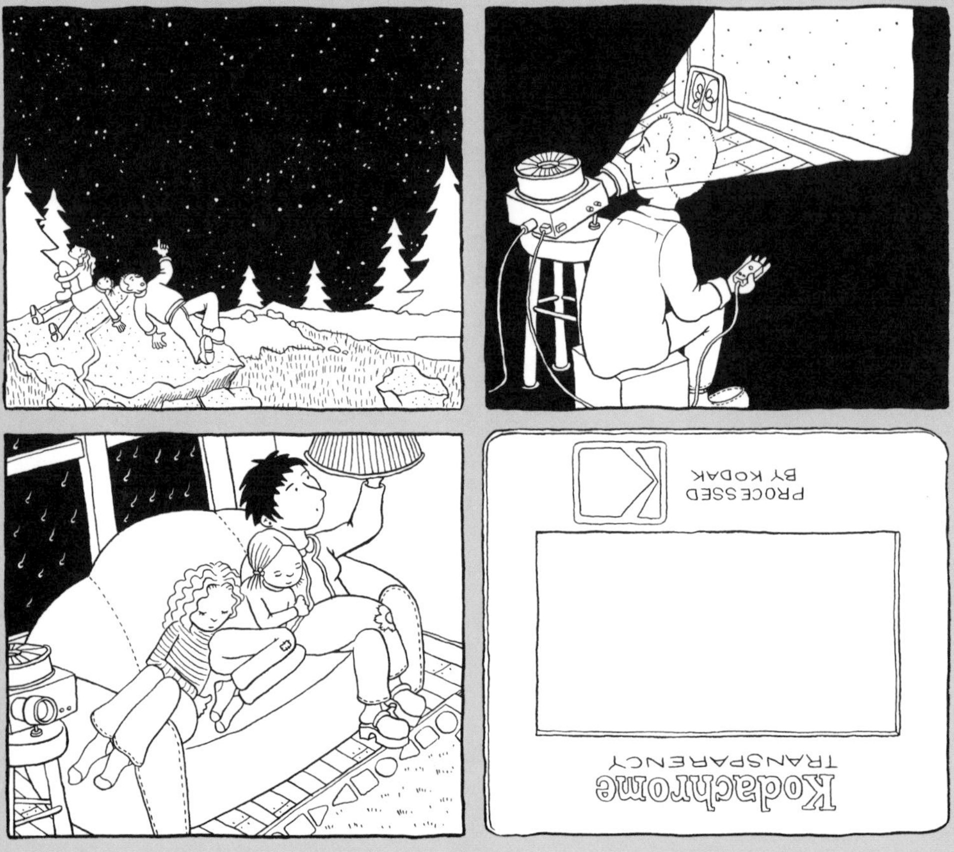
PROCESSED
BY KODAK
Kodachrome
TRANSPARENCY

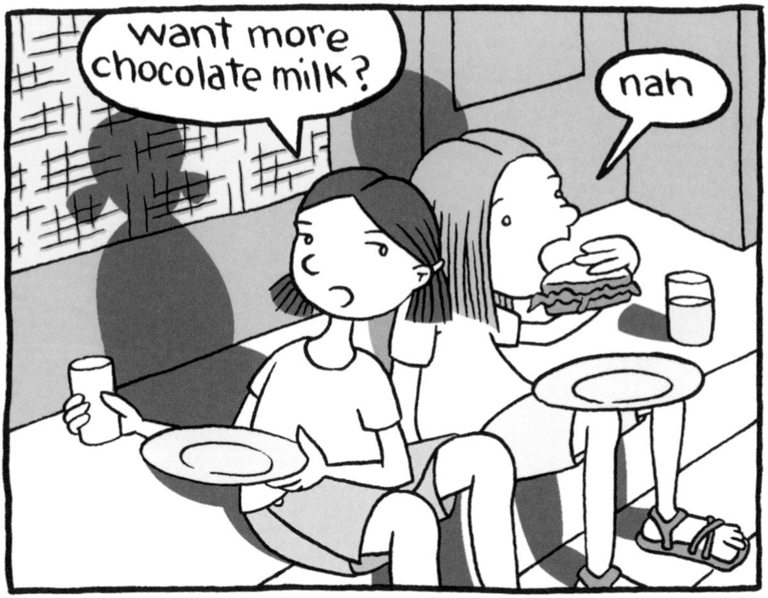
want more chocolate milk?
nah

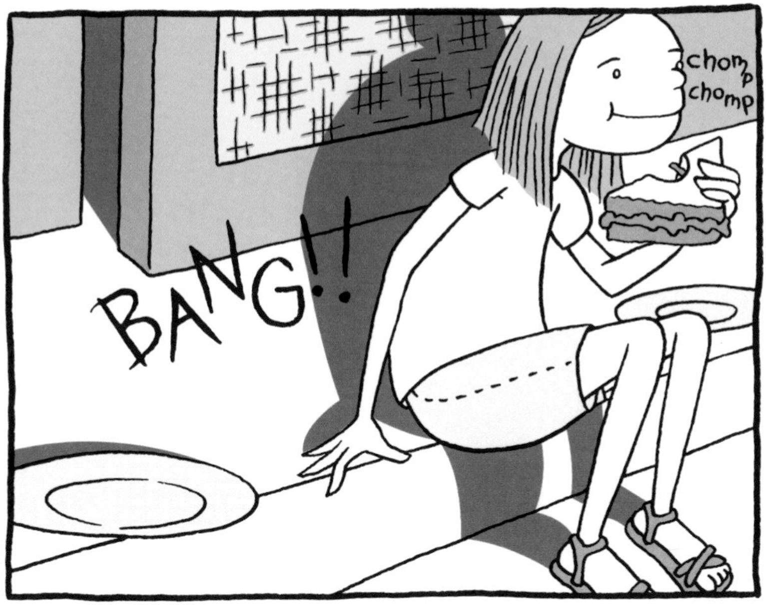
chomp chomp
BANG!!

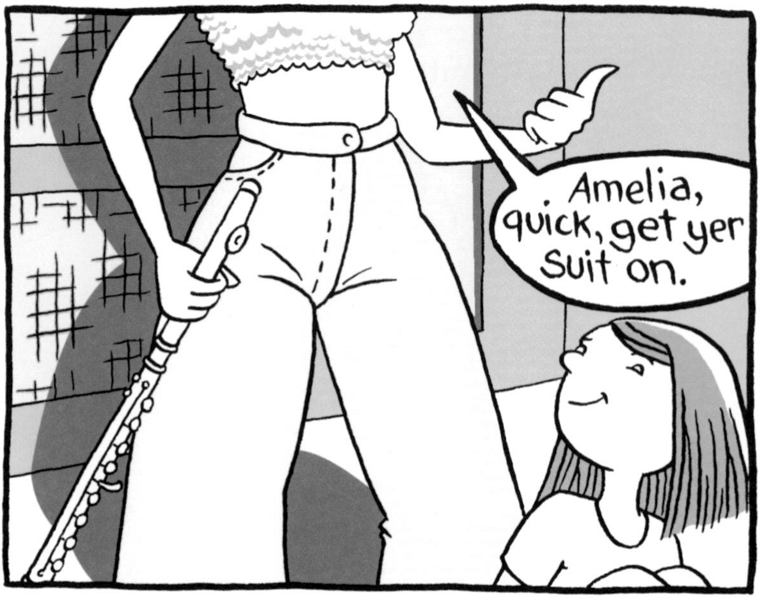
Amelia, quick, get yer suit on.

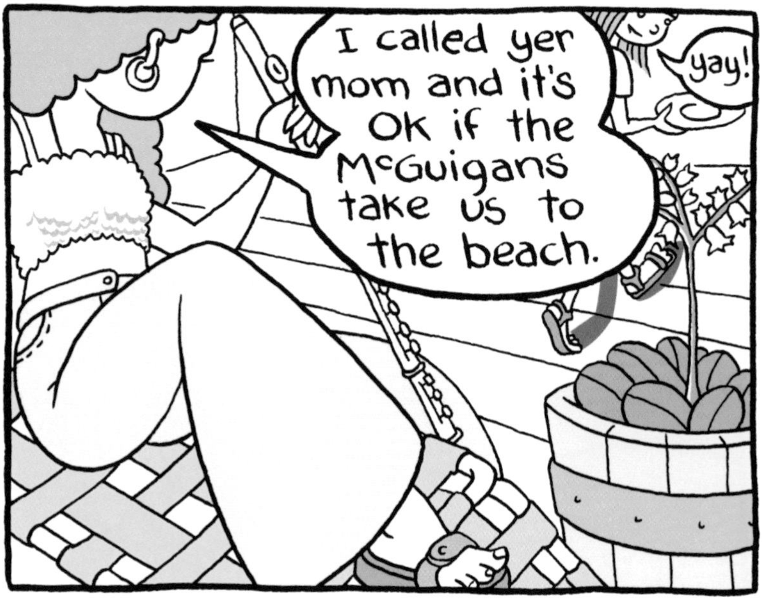
I called yer mom and it's OK if the McGuigans take us to the beach.
yay!

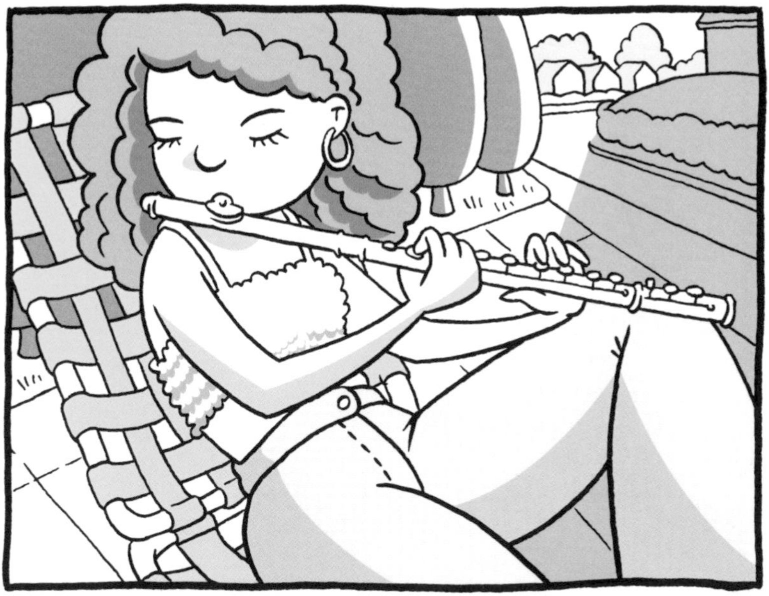

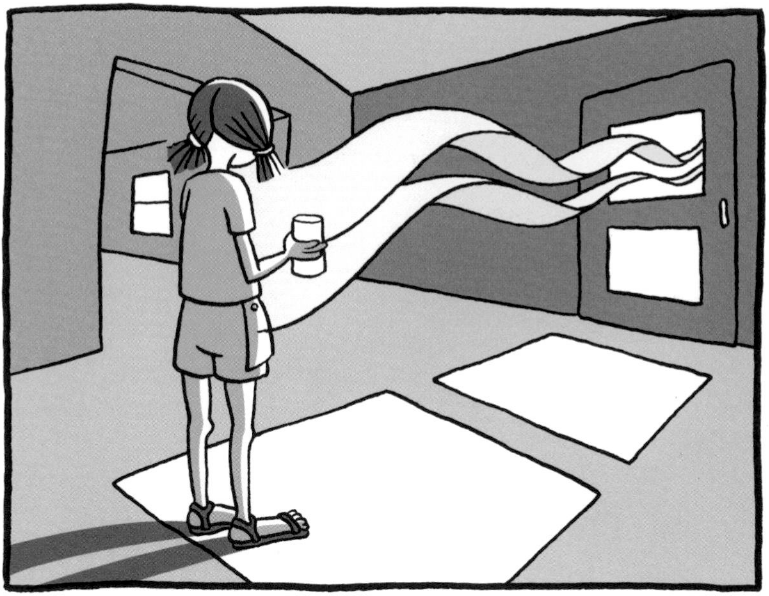

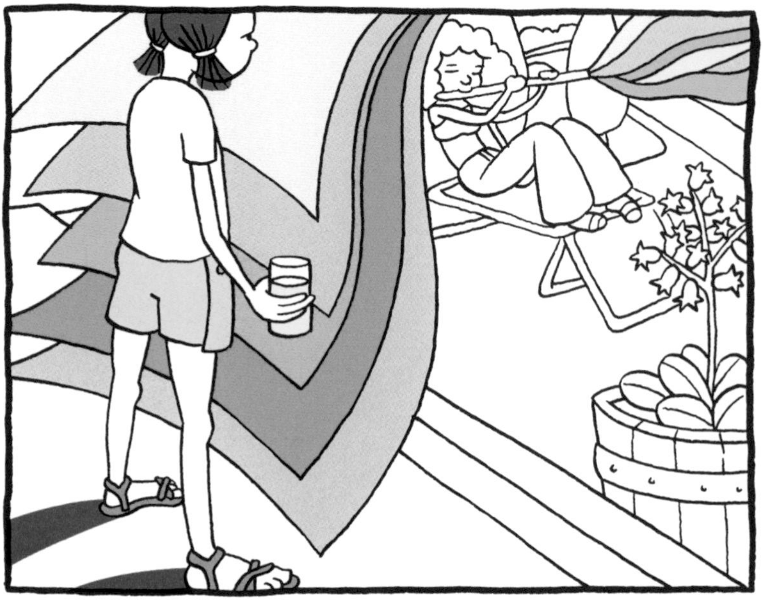

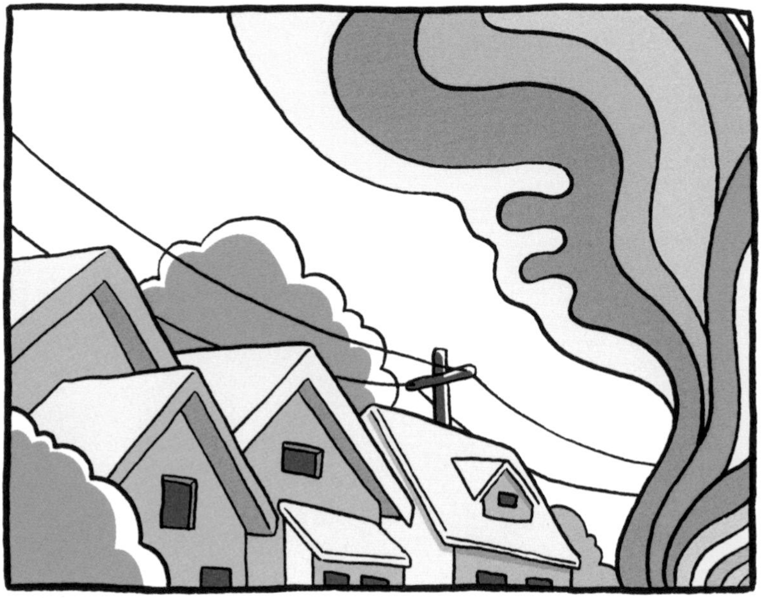

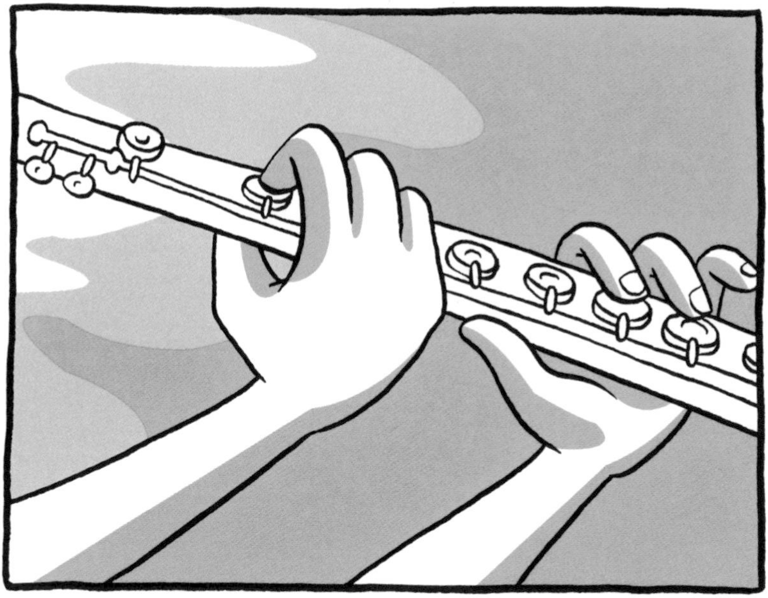

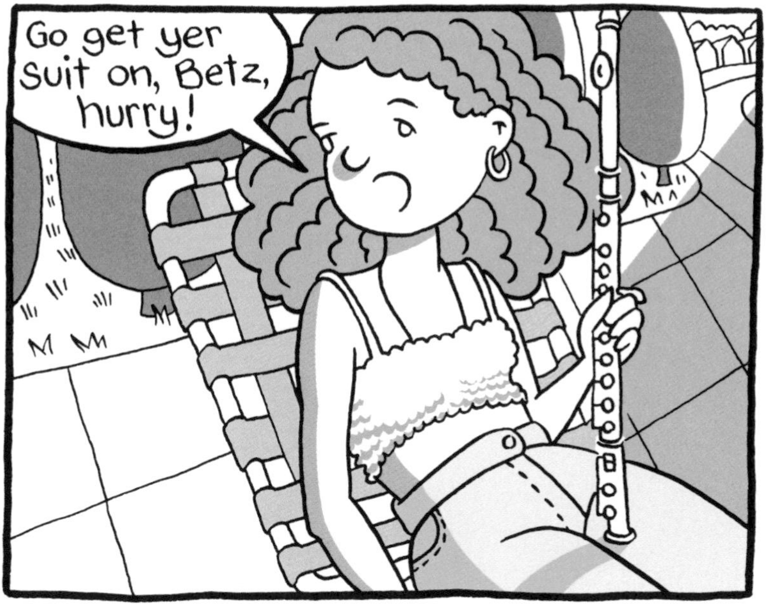
Go get yer suit on, Betz, hurry!

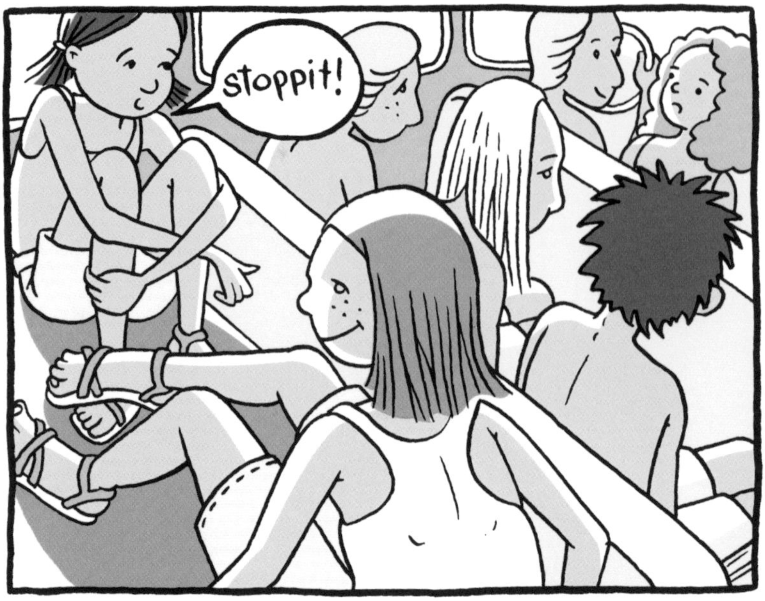
stoppit!

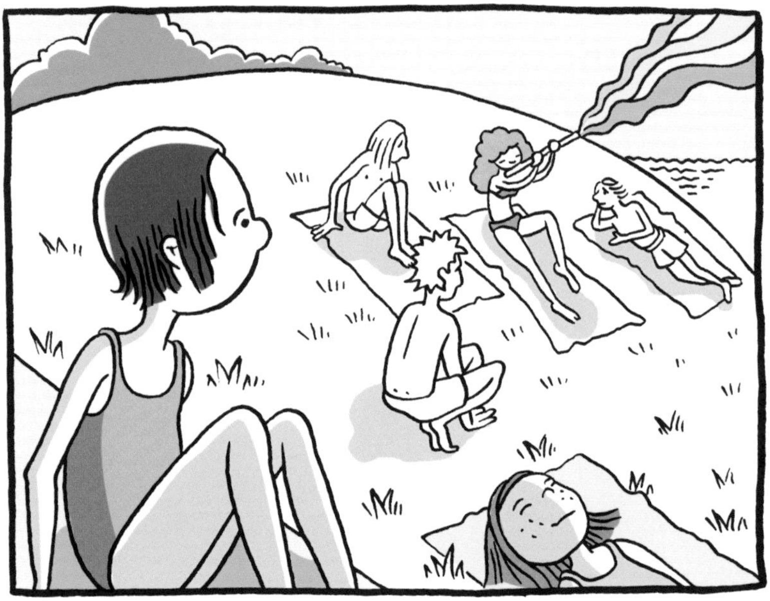

bills

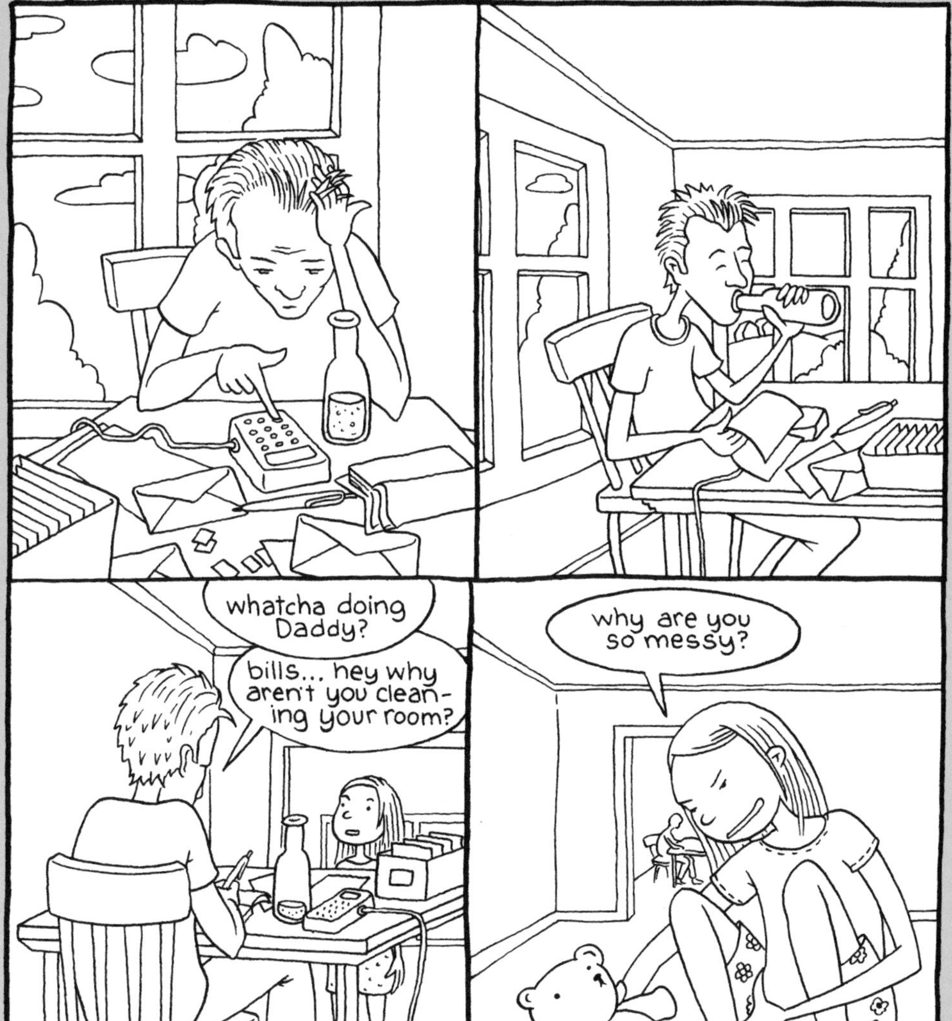
whatcha doing Daddy?
bills... hey why aren't you clean-ing your room?
why are you so messy?

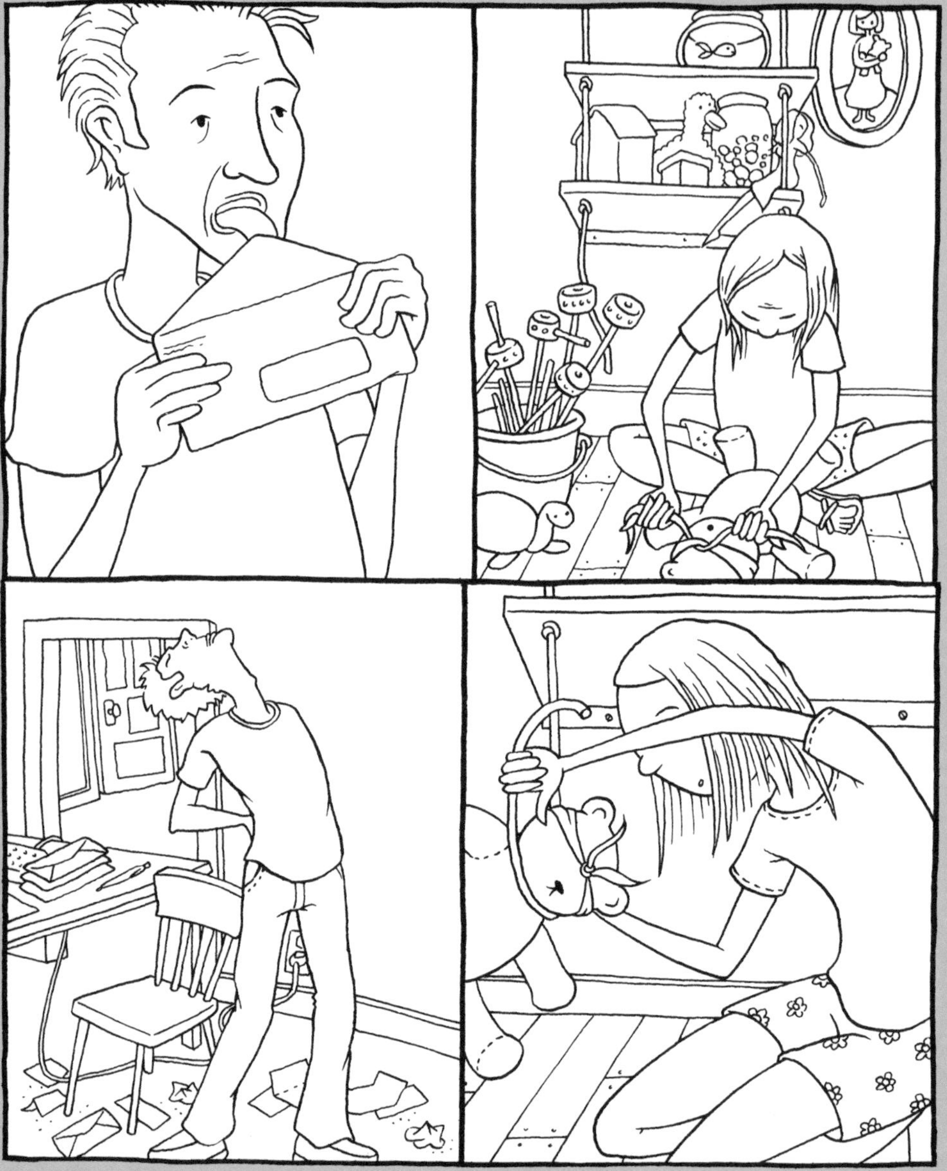

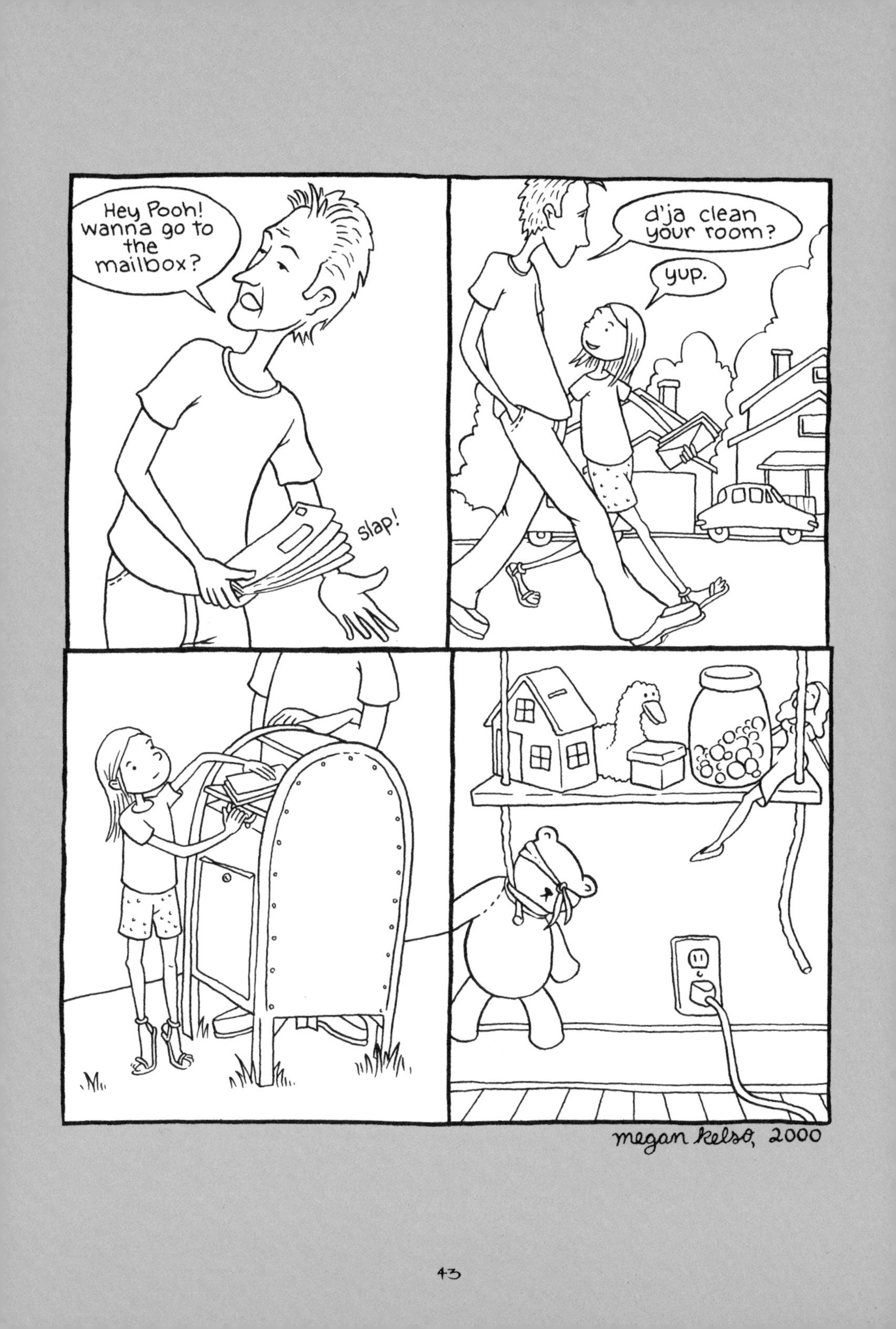
Hey Pooh! wanna go to the mailbox?
slap!
d'ja clean your room?
yup.
megan kelso, 2000

on the beautiful blue danube

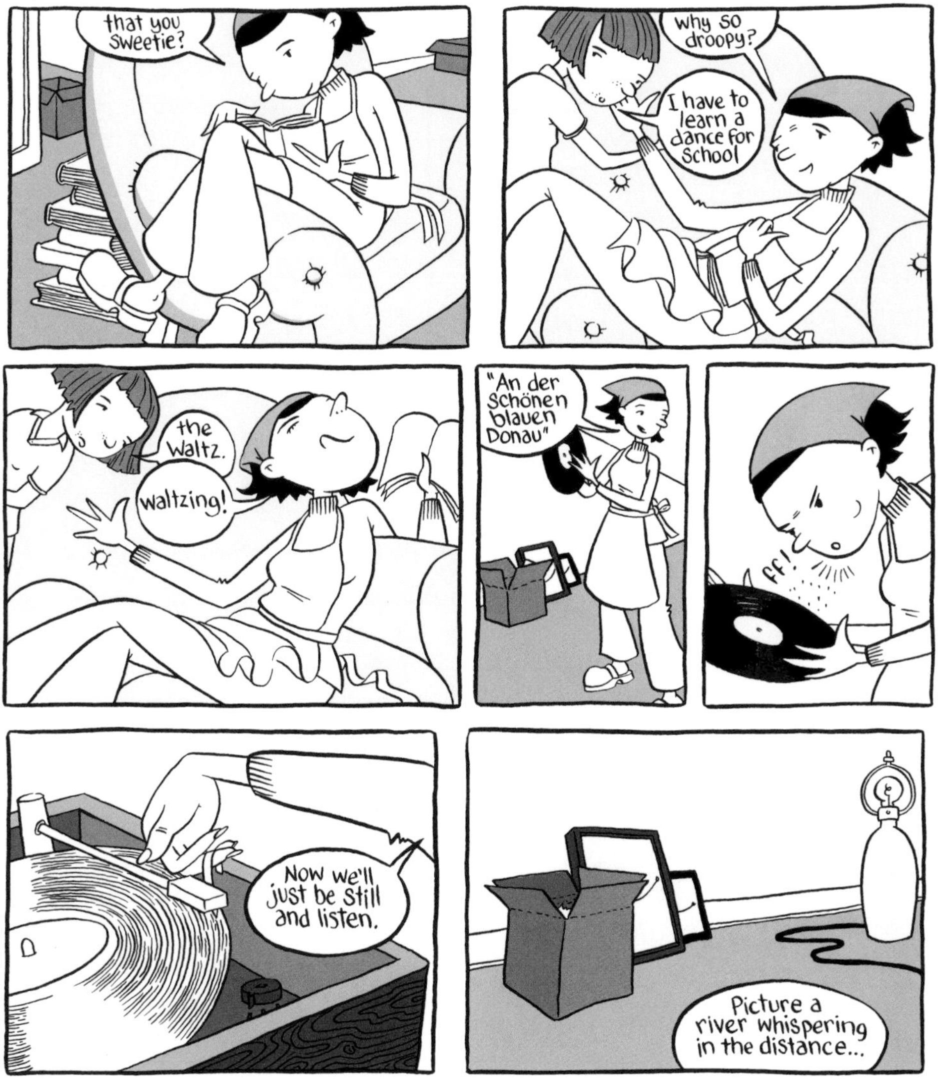

that you sweetie?
why so droopy?
I have to learn a dance for school
the Waltz.
waltzing!
"An der Schönen blauen Donau"
ff!
Now we'll just be still and listen.
Picture a river whispering in the distance...

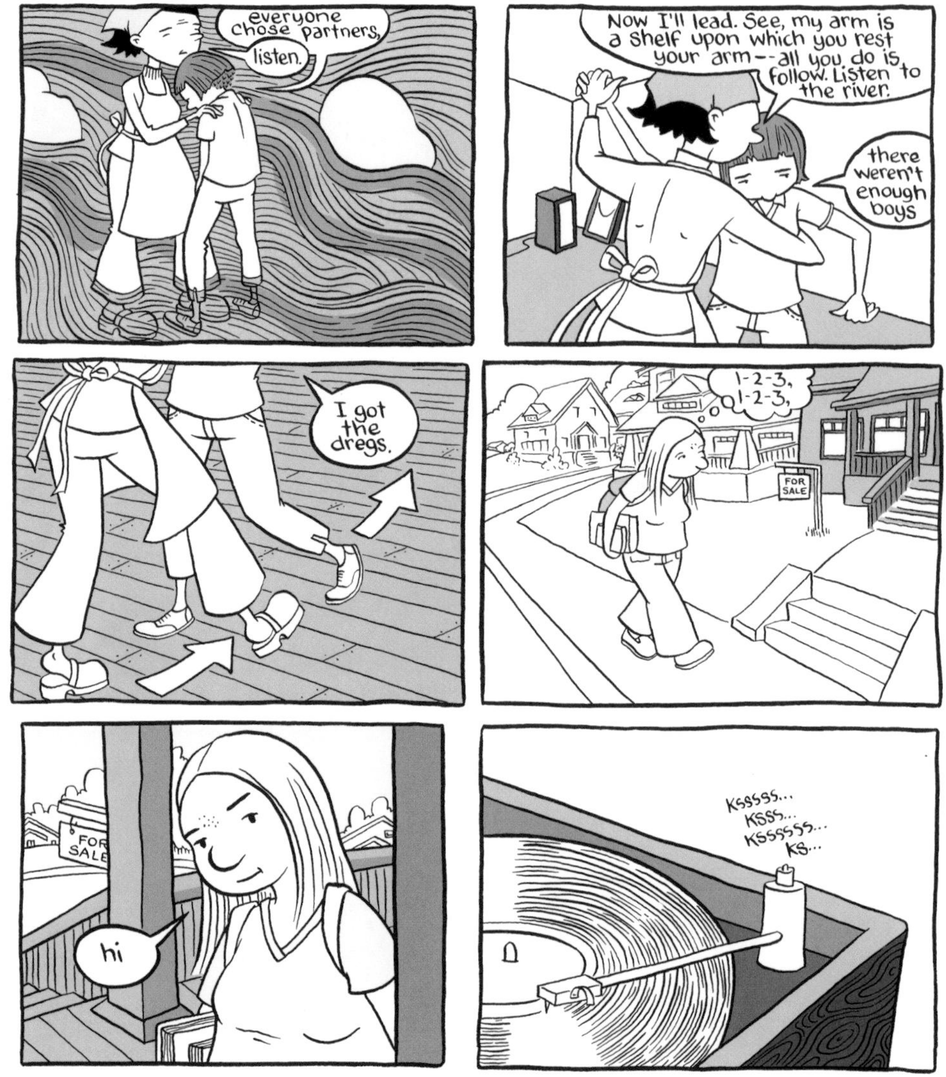
everyone chose partners,
listen.
Now I'll lead. See, my arm is a shelf upon which you rest your arm--all you do is follow. Listen to the river.
there weren't enough boys
I got the dregs.
1-2-3, 1-2-3,
FOR SALE
FOR SALE
hi
Kssssss... Ksss... Kssssss... Ks...

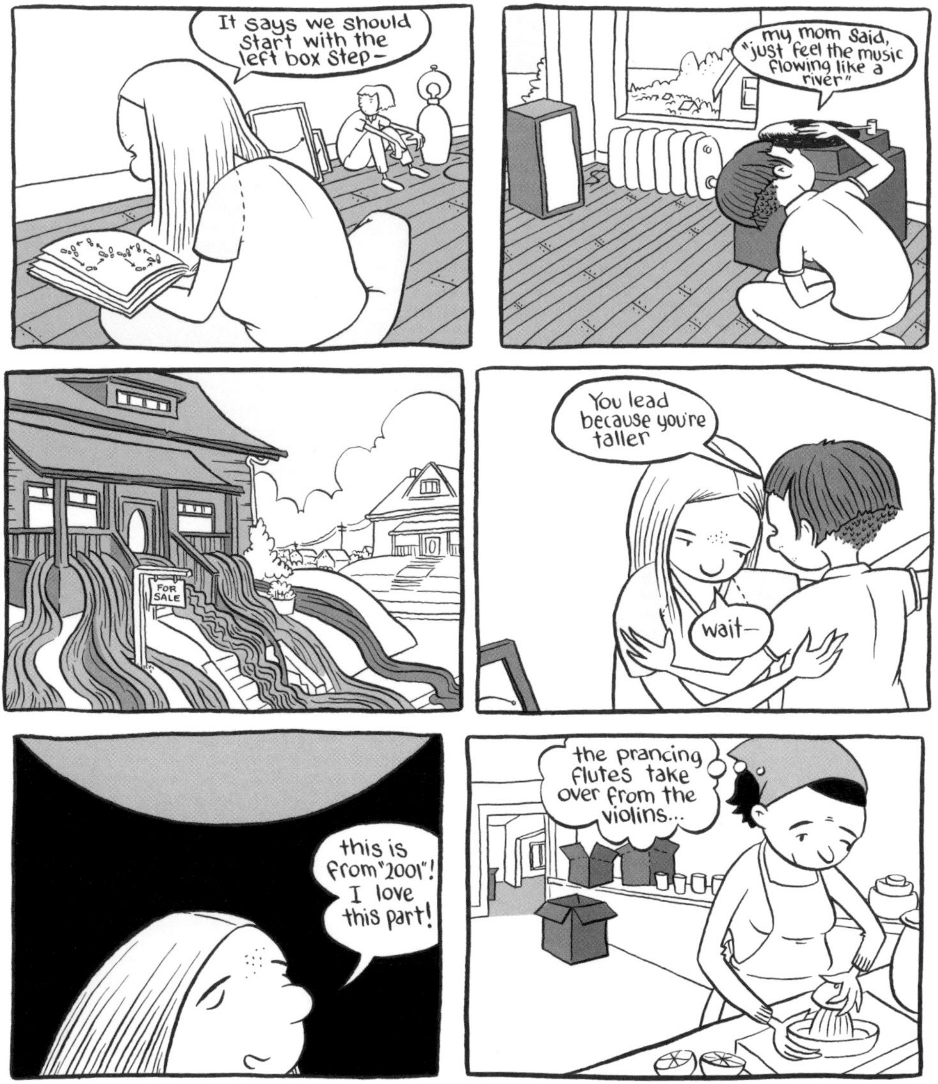
It says we should start with the left box step—
my mom said, "just feel the music flowing like a river"
FOR SALE
You lead because you're taller
wait—
this is from "2001"! I love this part!
the prancing flutes take over from the violins...

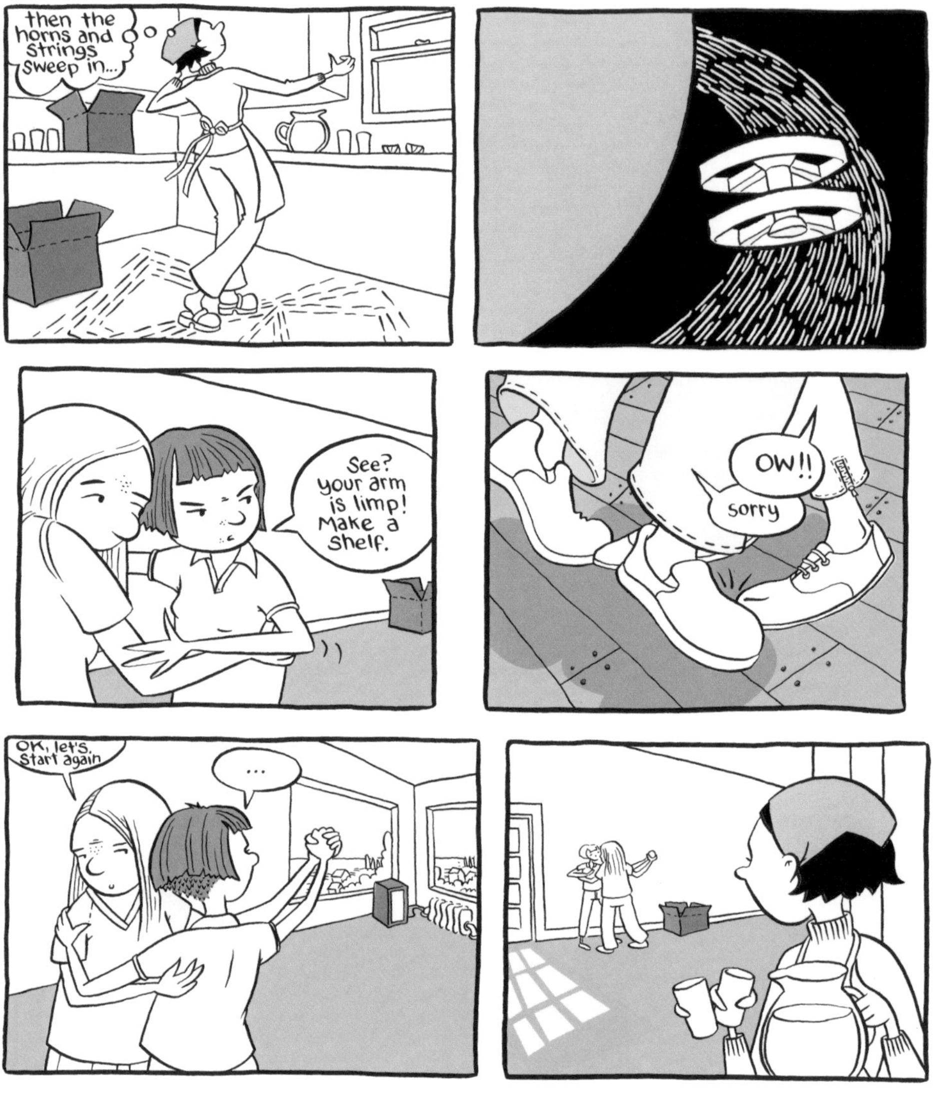

then the horns and strings sweep in...
See? your arm is limp! Make a shelf.
OW!!
sorry
OK, let's start again
...

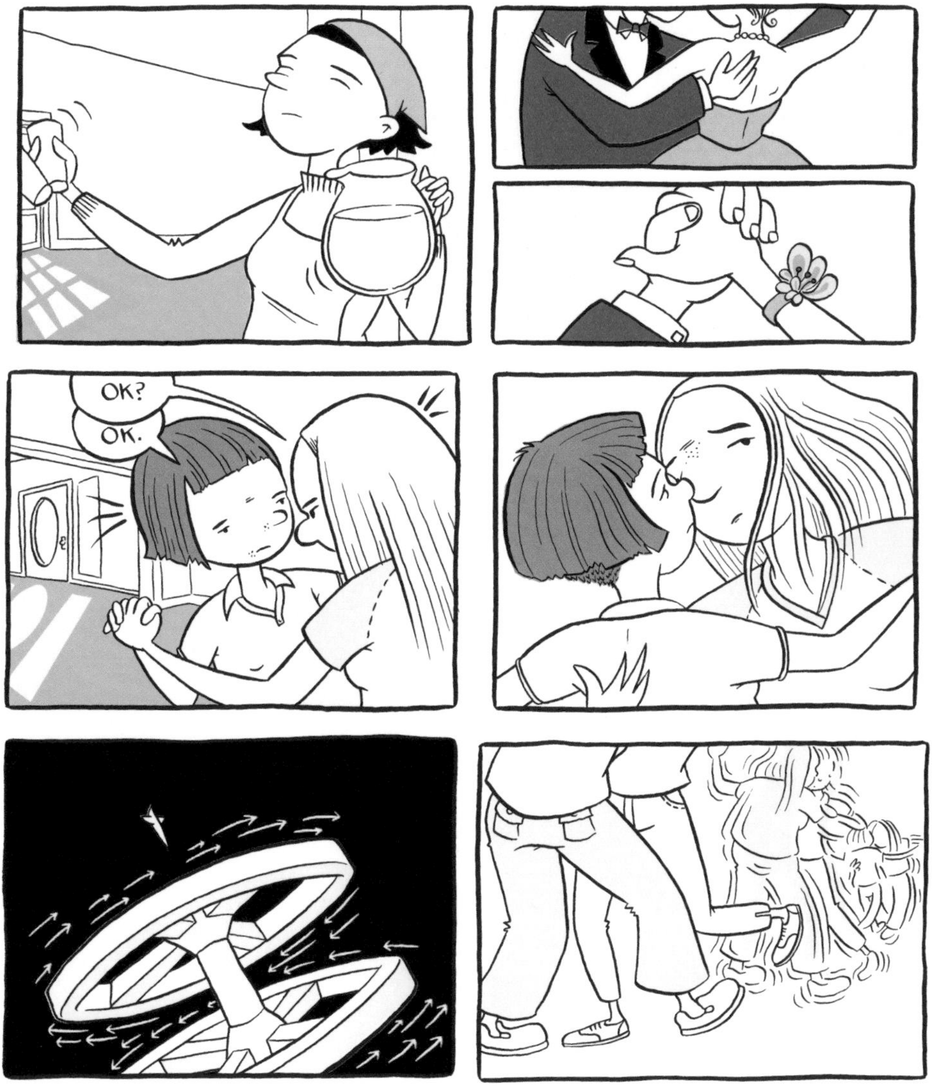
OK?
OK.

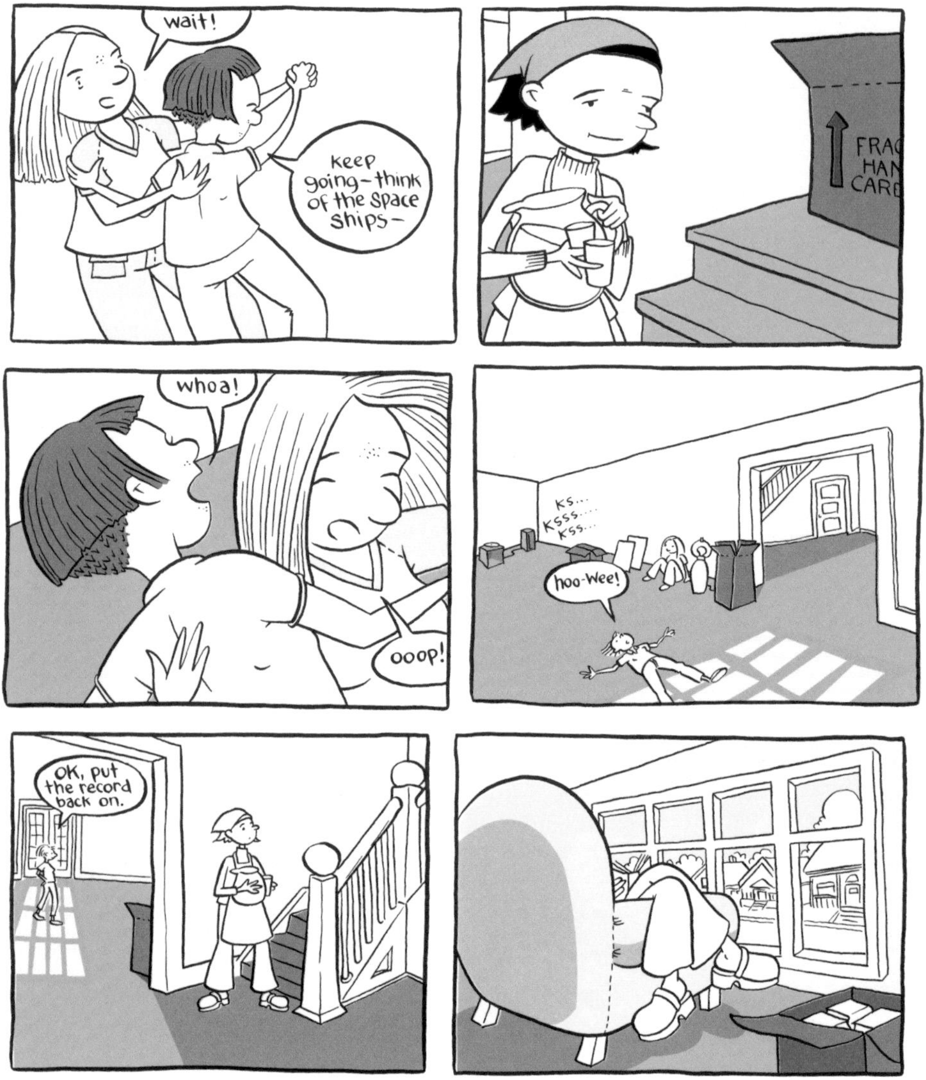
wait!
keep going—think of the space ships—
whoa!
ooop!
ks...
ksss...
kss...
hoo-Wee!
OK, put the record back on.

megan kelso ©2002

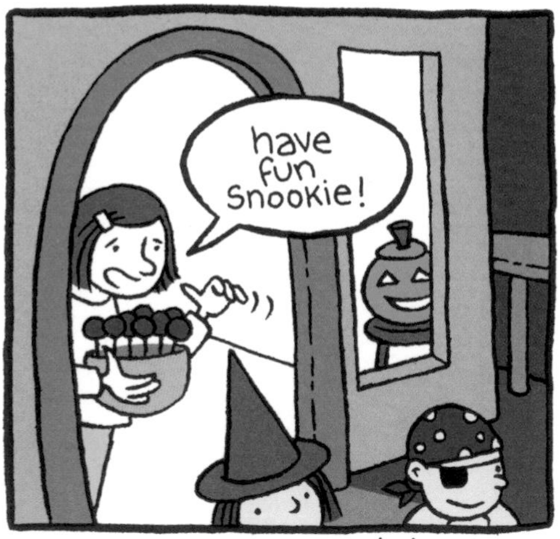
have fun Snookie!

You learn a lot trick-or-treating...

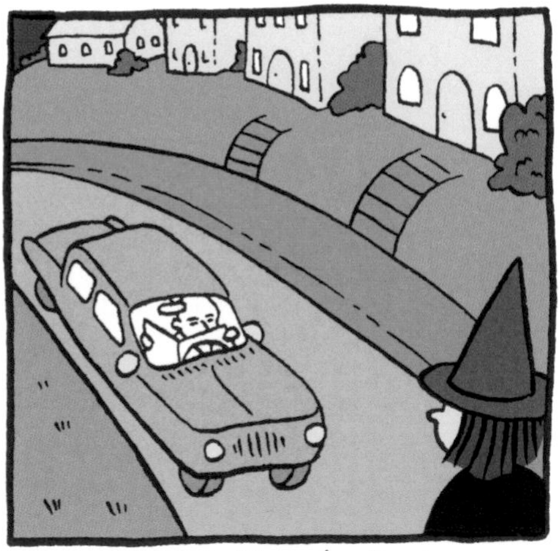

Mr. Collins hated Halloween.

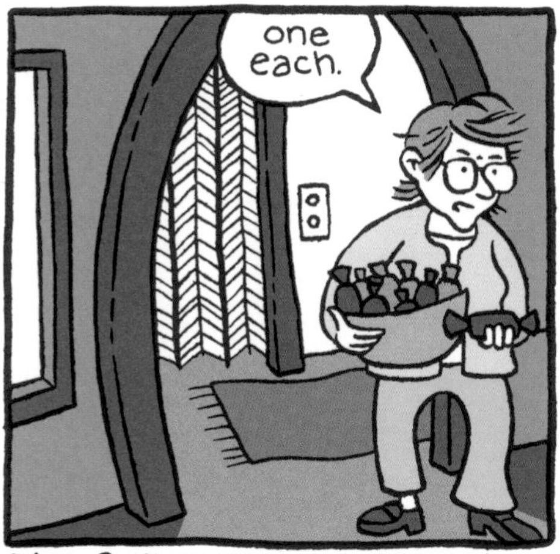
one each.

Mrs. Collins smelled like cat litter and they had an elevator (why)?

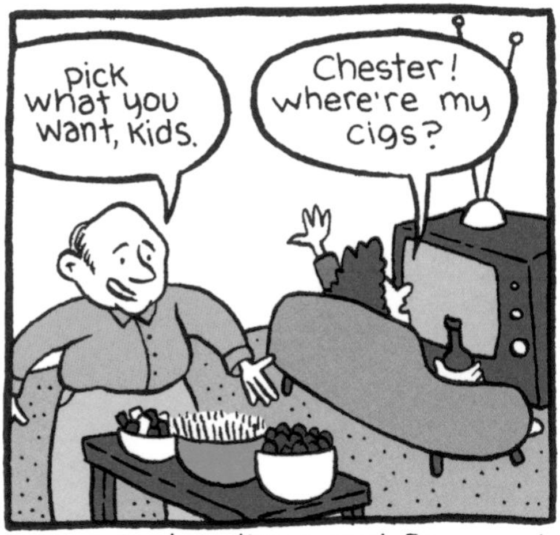
Pick what you want, kids.
Chester! where're my cigs?

Mr. Winston liked Neil Diamond, but Mrs. Winston didn't.

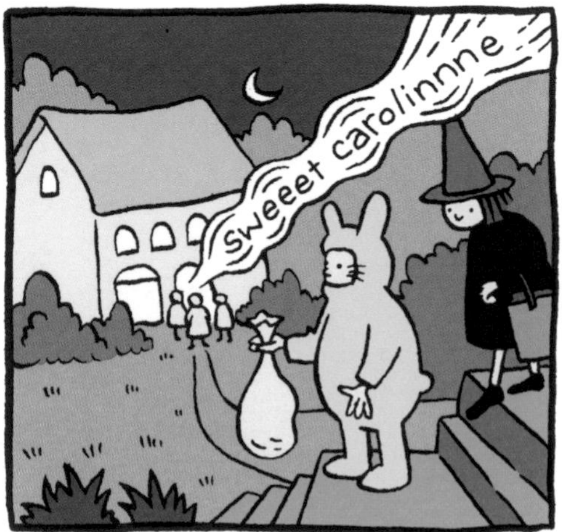
sweeet carolinnne

Mrs. McAllister liked
Neil Diamond too.

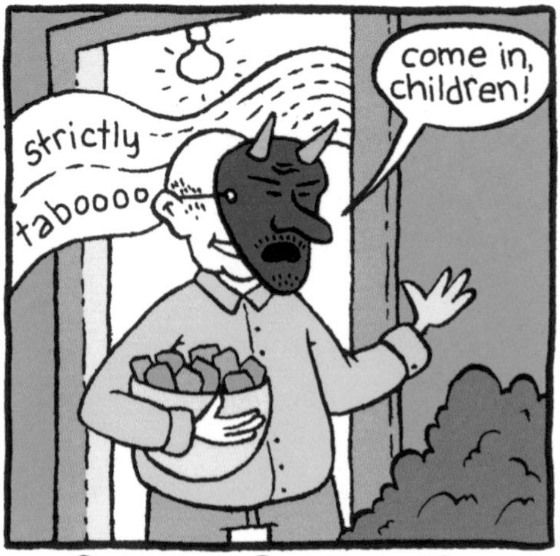
strictly
taboooo
come in, children!

Grandpa Rowkowski
favored Sinatra.

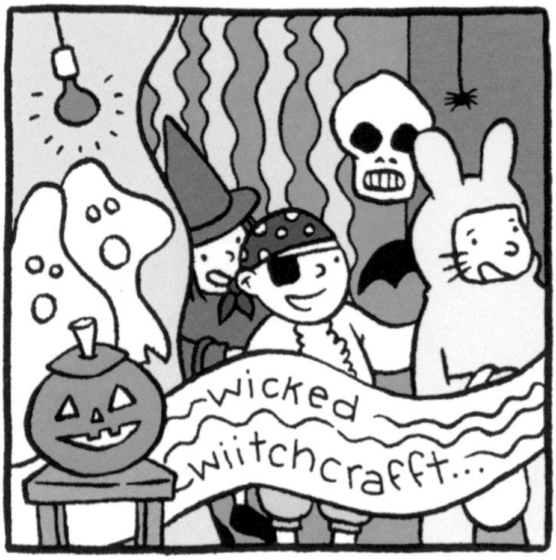
wicked
wiitchcrafft...

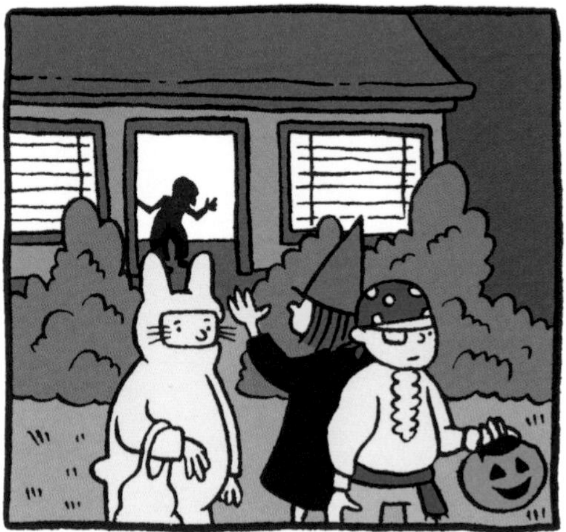

We visited Grandpa at
non-Halloween times too,
but mostly we stole his flowers.

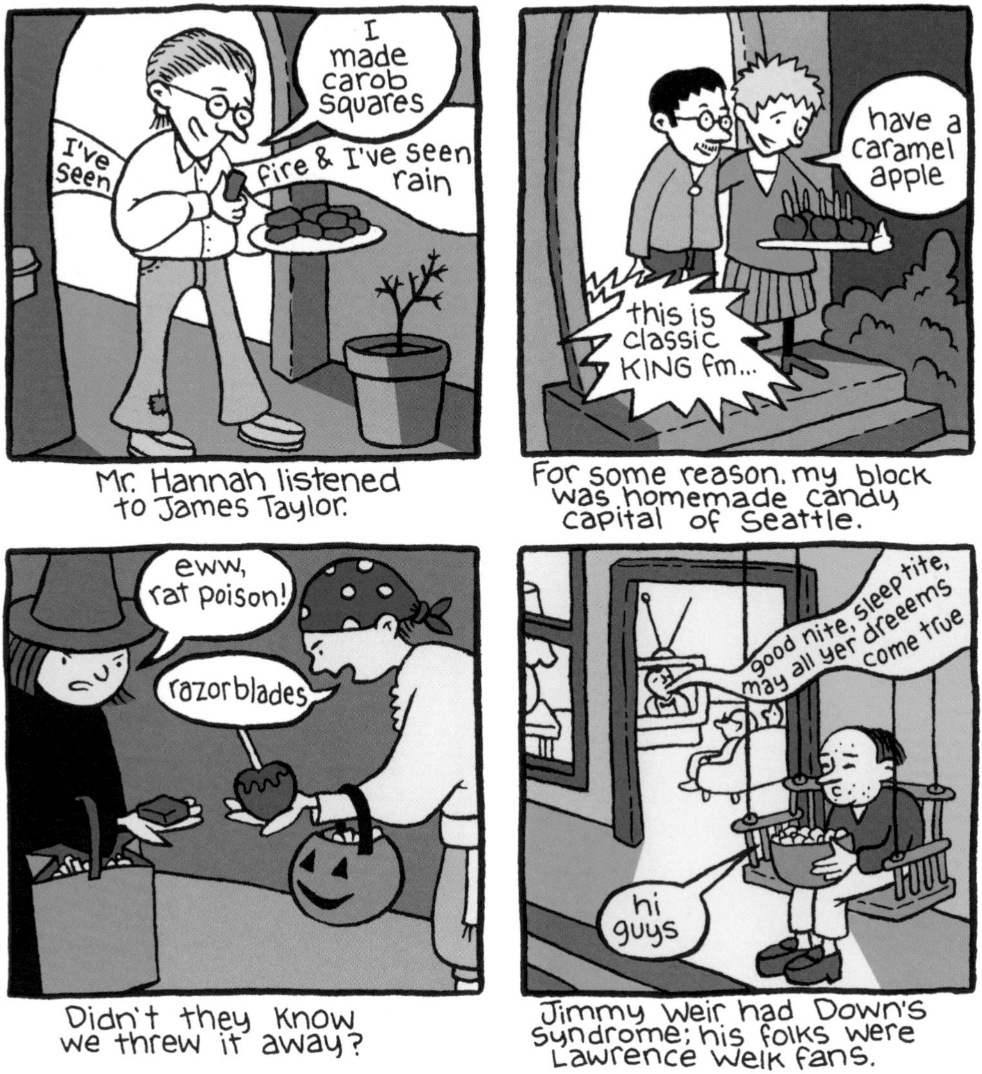
I made carob squares
I've seen fire & I've seen rain
Mr. Hannah listened to James Taylor.
have a caramel apple
this is classic KING fm...
For some reason, my block was homemade candy capital of Seattle.
eww, rat poison!
razorblades
Didn't they know we threw it away?
good nite, sleep tite, may all yer dreeems come true
hi guys
Jimmy Weir had Down's syndrome; his folks were Lawrence Welk fans.

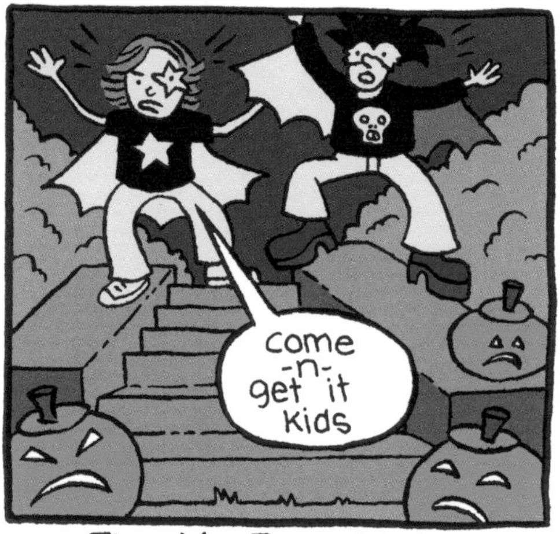
come -n- get it kids
The MacDougal twins blasted Kiss

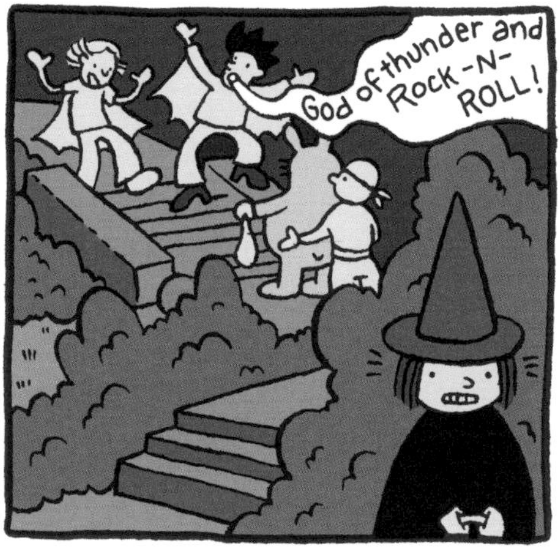
God of thunder and ROCK-N-ROLL!

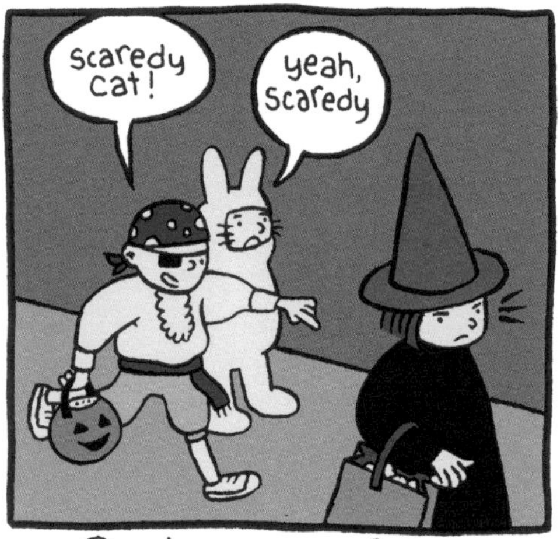
scaredy cat!
yeah, scaredy
Our bags were full.

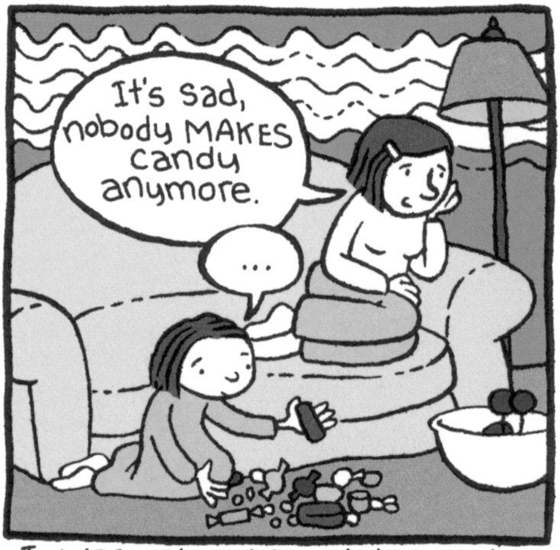
It's sad, nobody MAKES candy anymore.
...
I was glad to get home to Mom: lollipops made from scratch & Pachabel's Canon in D.

the Pickle Fork
Your family owns the biggest factory in Pickle City—
Willard Pickles
and I am a tacky, little nothing.
I am in love, I can have any-thing I want. I want you.
Oh, Mr. Willard!
Collectors like your husband are the real heroes, Mrs. Willard, I'm only a curator.

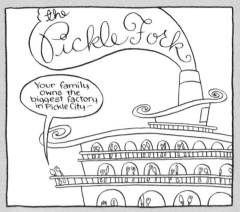

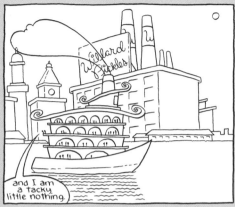

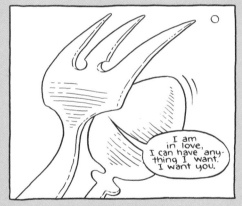

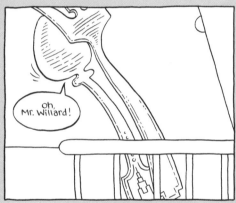

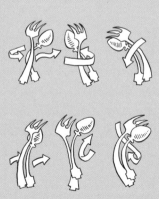

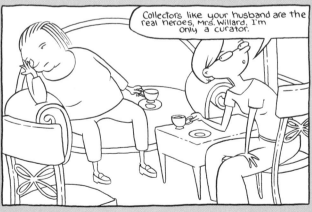

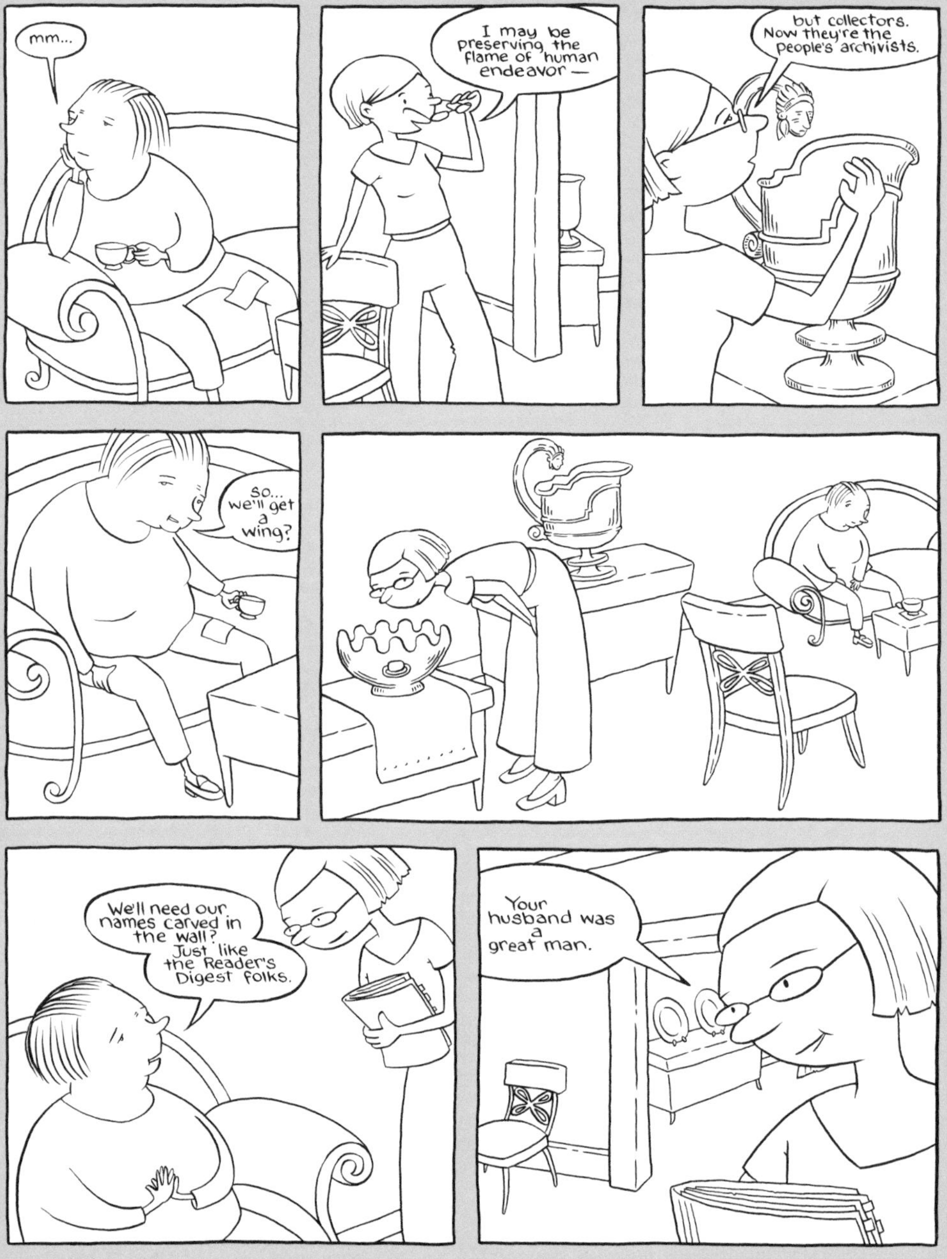
mm...
I may be preserving the flame of human endeavor —
but collectors. Now they're the people's archivists.
so... we'll get a wing?
We'll need our names carved in the wall? Just like the Reader's Digest folks.
Your husband was a great man.

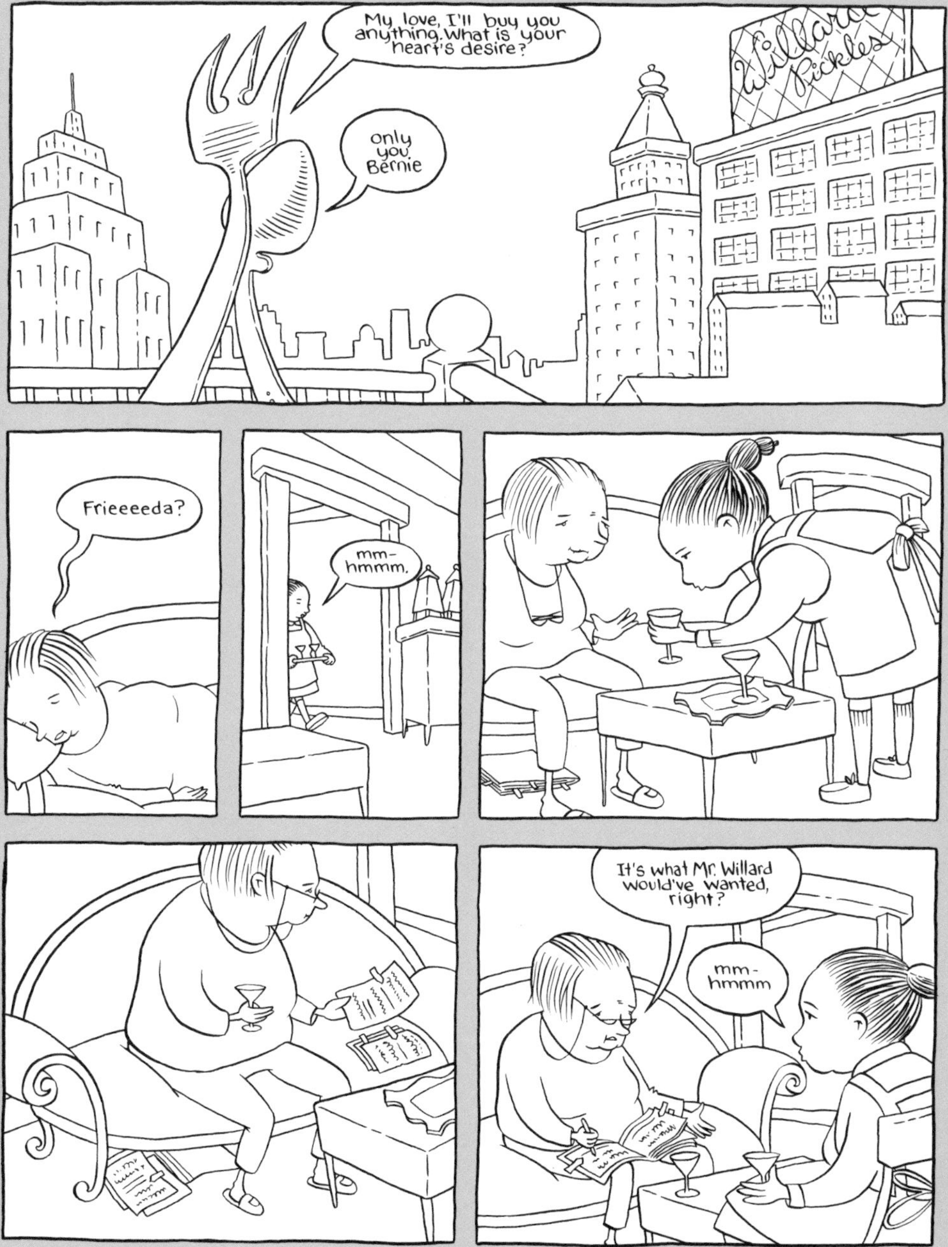
My love, I'll buy you anything. What is your heart's desire?
only you, Bernie
Willard Pickles
Frieeeeda?
mm-hmmm.
It's what Mr. Willard would've wanted, right?
mm-hmmm

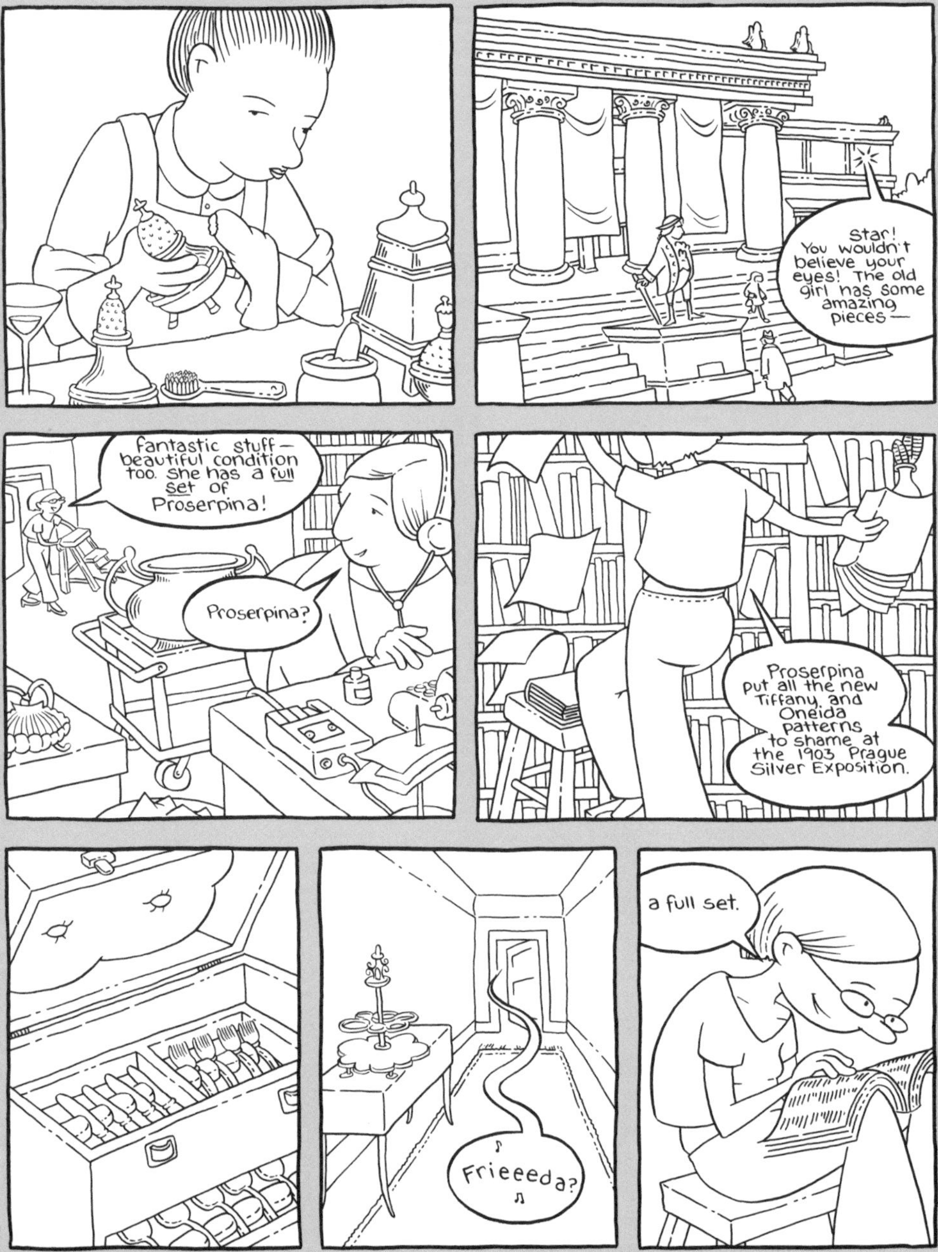
Star! You wouldn't believe your eyes! The old girl has some amazing pieces—
fantastic stuff—beautiful condition too. She has a full set of Proserpina!
Proserpina?
Proserpina put all the new Tiffany, and Oneida patterns to shame at the 1903 Prague Silver Exposition.
Frieeeda?
a full set.

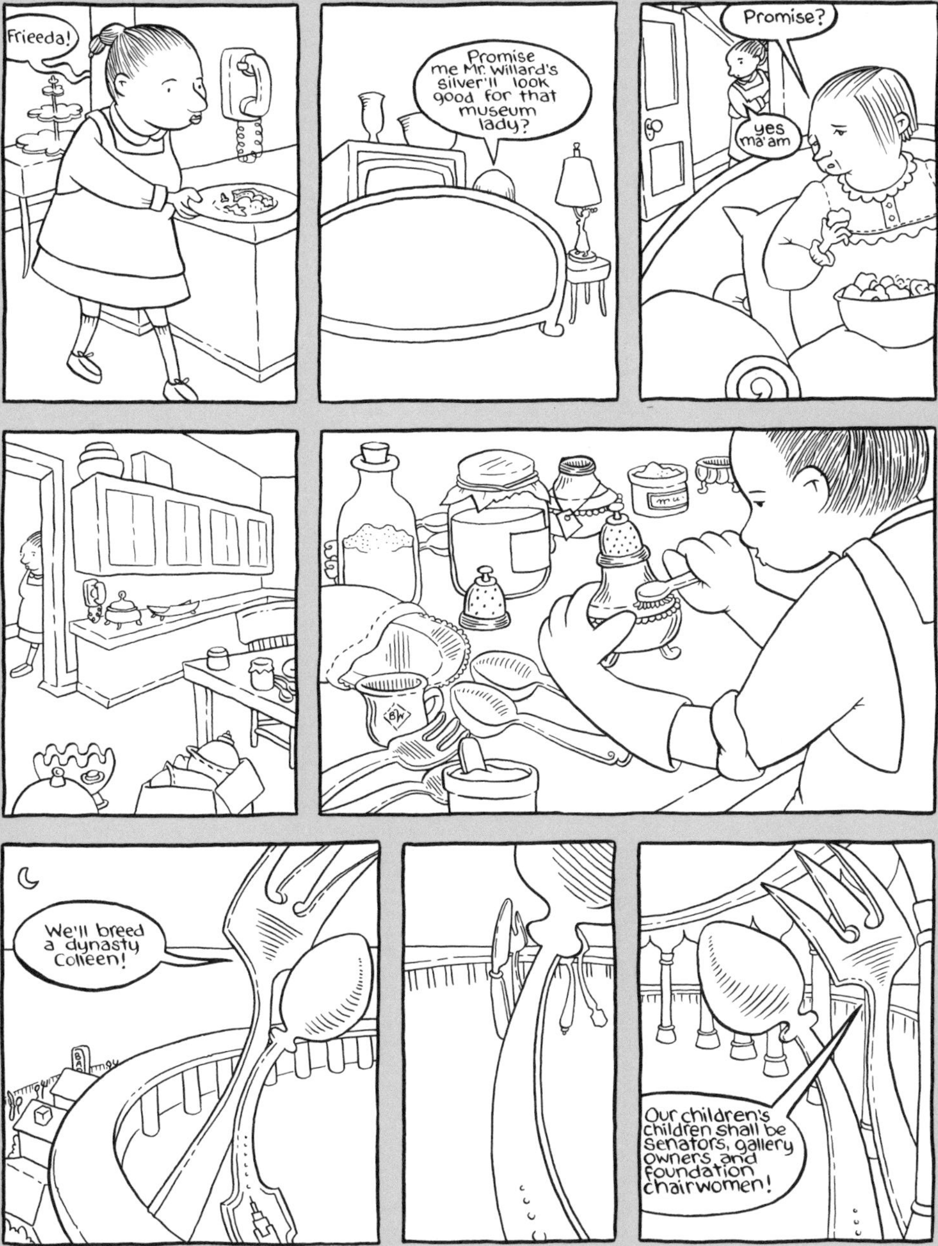
Frieeda!
Promise me Mr. Willard's silver'll look good for that museum lady?
Promise?
yes ma'am
We'll breed a dynasty Colleen!
Our children's children shall be senators, gallery owners and foundation chairwomen!

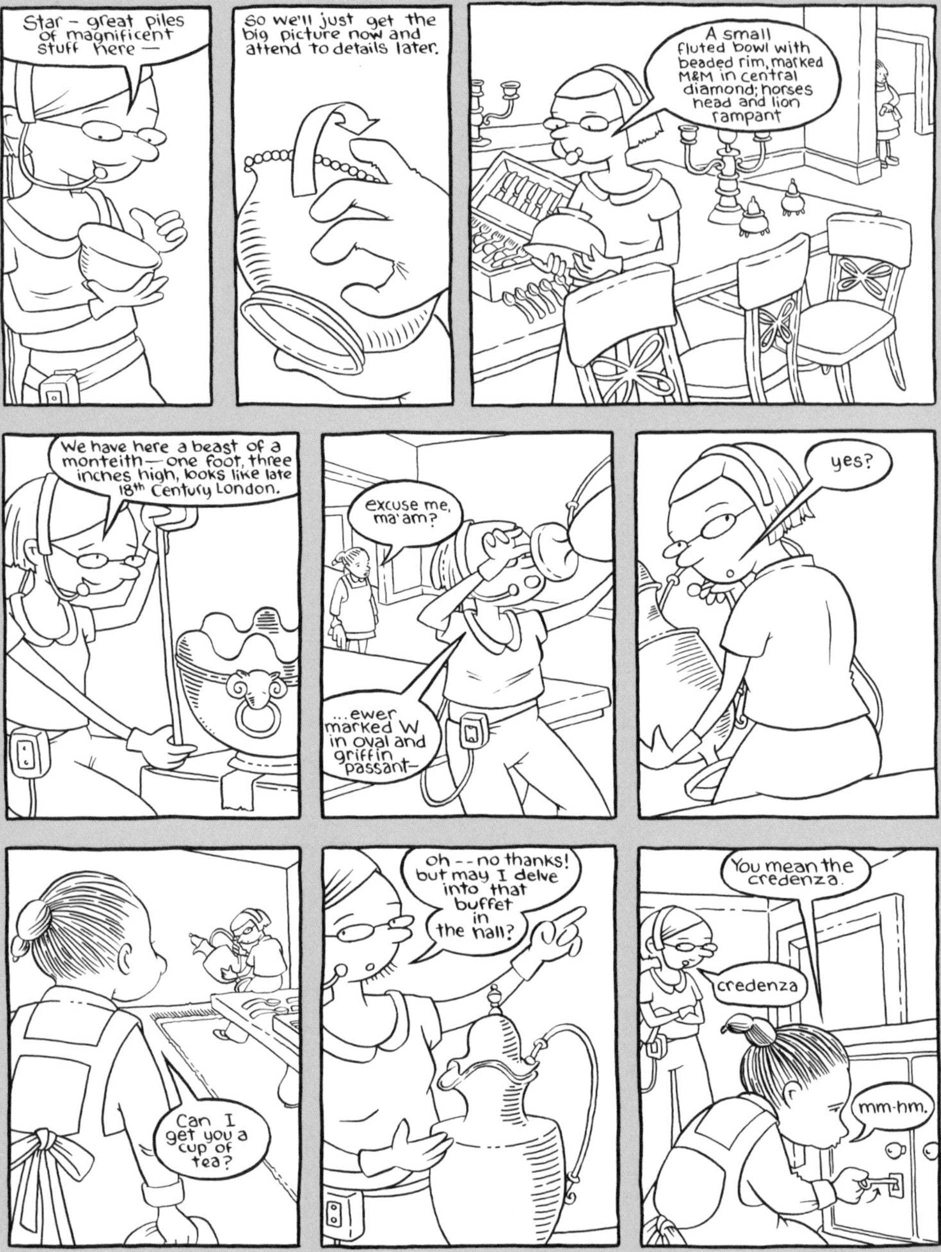

Star - great piles of magnificent stuff here —
So we'll just get the big picture now and attend to details later.
A small fluted bowl with beaded rim, marked M&M in central diamond; horses head and lion rampant
We have here a beast of a monteith — one foot, three inches high, looks like late 18th Century London.
excuse me, ma'am?
...ewer marked W in oval and griffin passant-
yes?
Can I get you a cup of tea?
oh -- no thanks! but may I delve into that buffet in the hall?
You mean the credenza.
credenza
mm-hm.

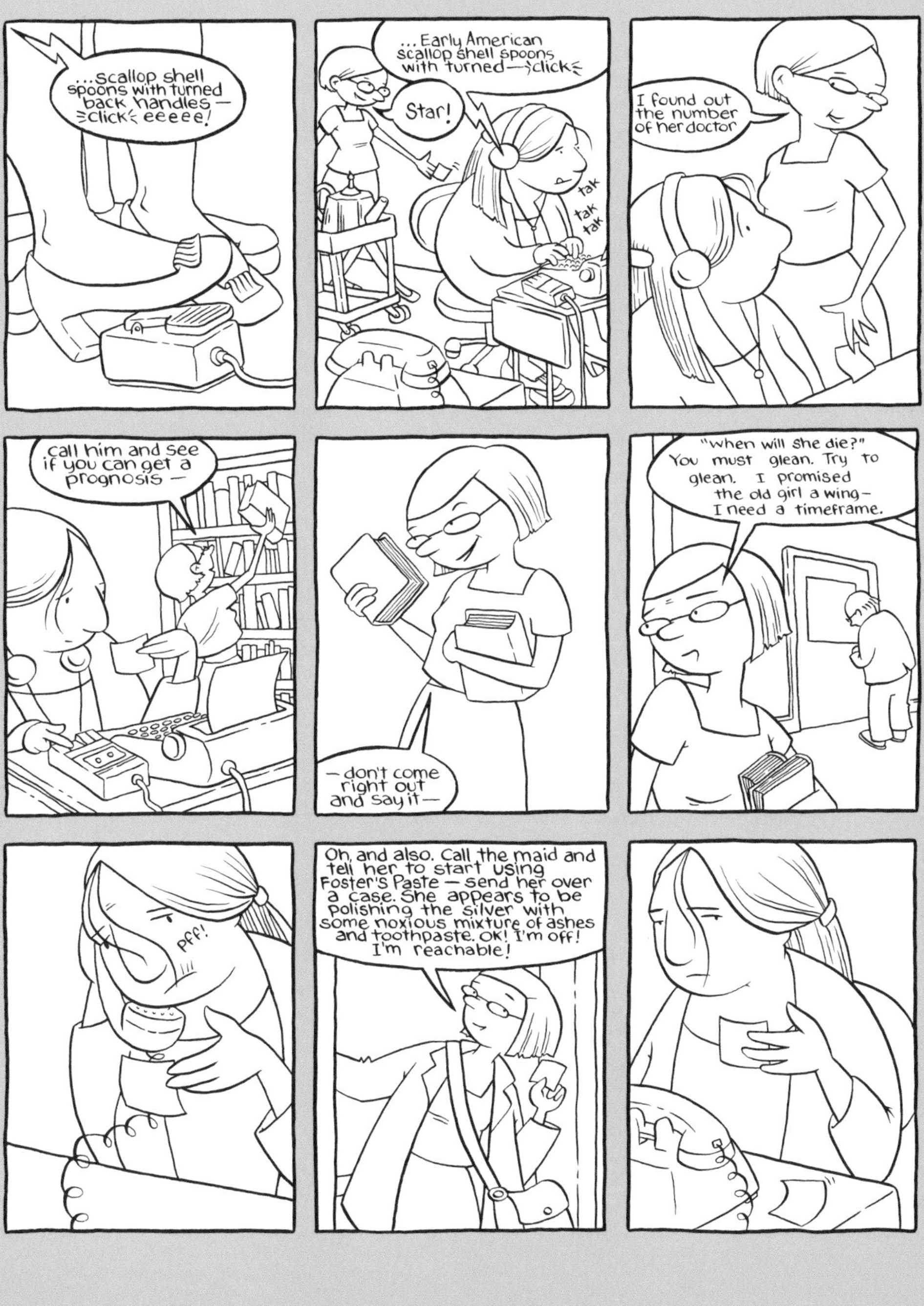

...Scallop shell spoons with turned back handles — ≶click≶ eeeee!
...Early American scallop shell spoons with turned —≶click≶
Star!
tak tak tak
I found out the number of her doctor
call him and see if you can get a prognosis —
— don't come right out and say it —
"when will she die?" You must glean. Try to glean. I promised the old girl a wing— I need a timeframe.
pff!
Oh, and also. Call the maid and tell her to start using Foster's Paste — send her over a case. She appears to be polishing the silver with some noxious mixture of ashes and toothpaste. OK! I'm off! I'm reachable!

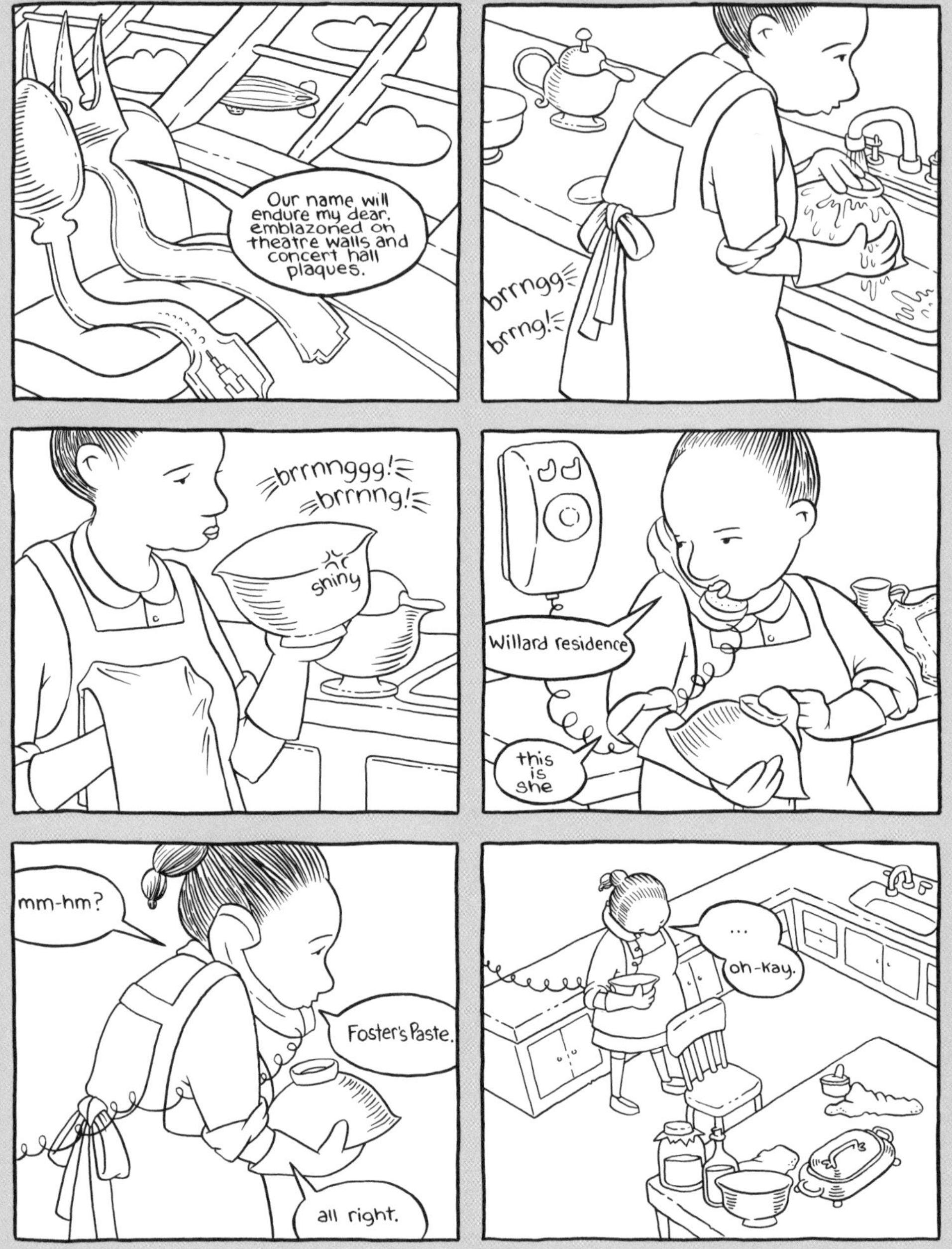
Our name will endure my dear, emblazoned on theatre walls and concert hall plaques.
brrngg
brrng!
brrnnggg!
brrnng!
shiny
Willard residence
this is she
mm-hm?
Foster's Paste.
all right.
...
oh-kay.

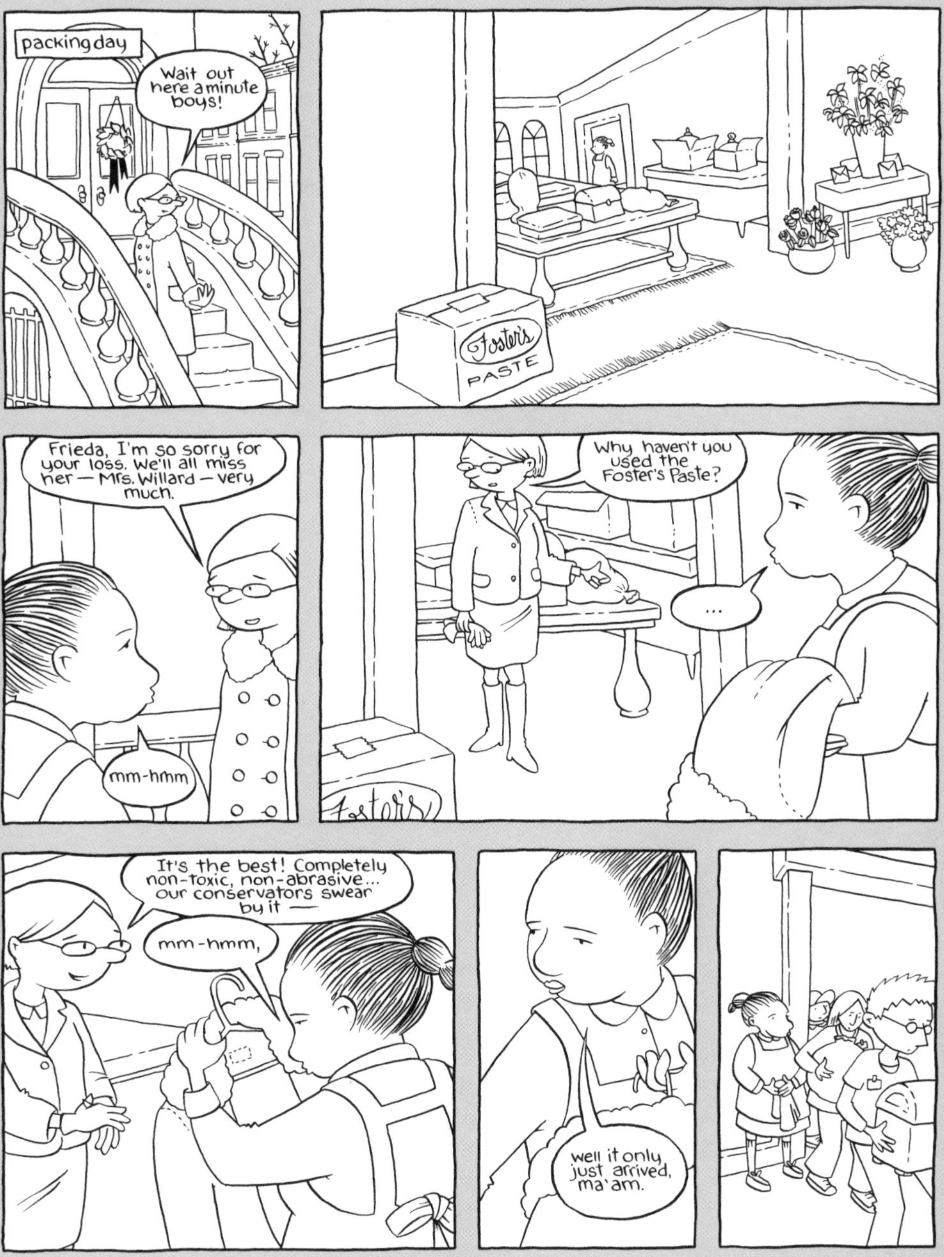
packing day
Wait out here a minute boys!
Foster's PASTE
Frieda, I'm so sorry for your loss. We'll all miss her — Mrs. Willard — very much.
mm-hmm
Why haven't you used the Foster's Paste?
...
Foster's
It's the best! Completely non-toxic, non-abrasive... our conservators swear by it —
mm-hmm,
well it only just arrived, ma'am.

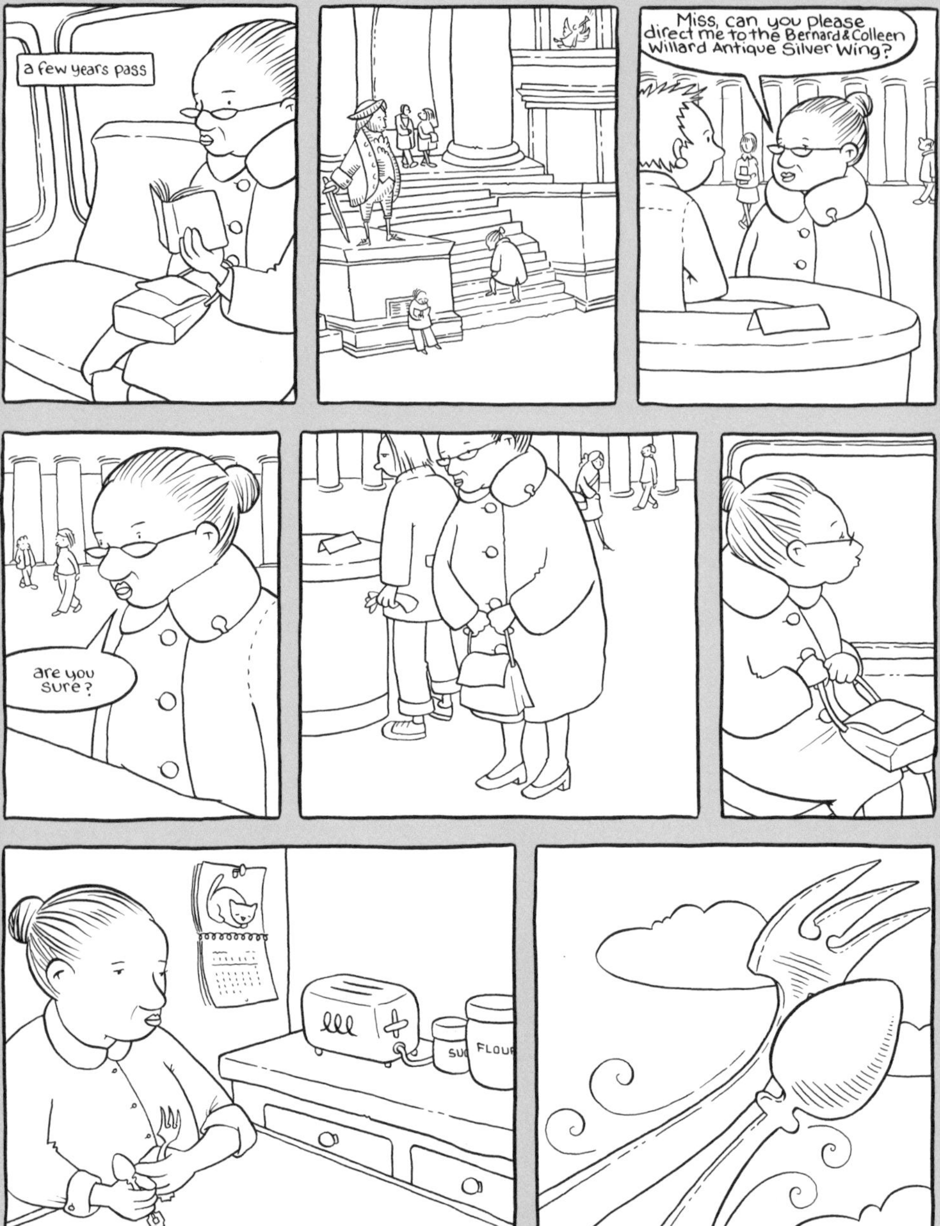

a few years pass
Miss, can you please direct me to the Bernard & Colleen Willard Antique Silver Wing?
are you sure?
SUG
FLOUR

Meow Face

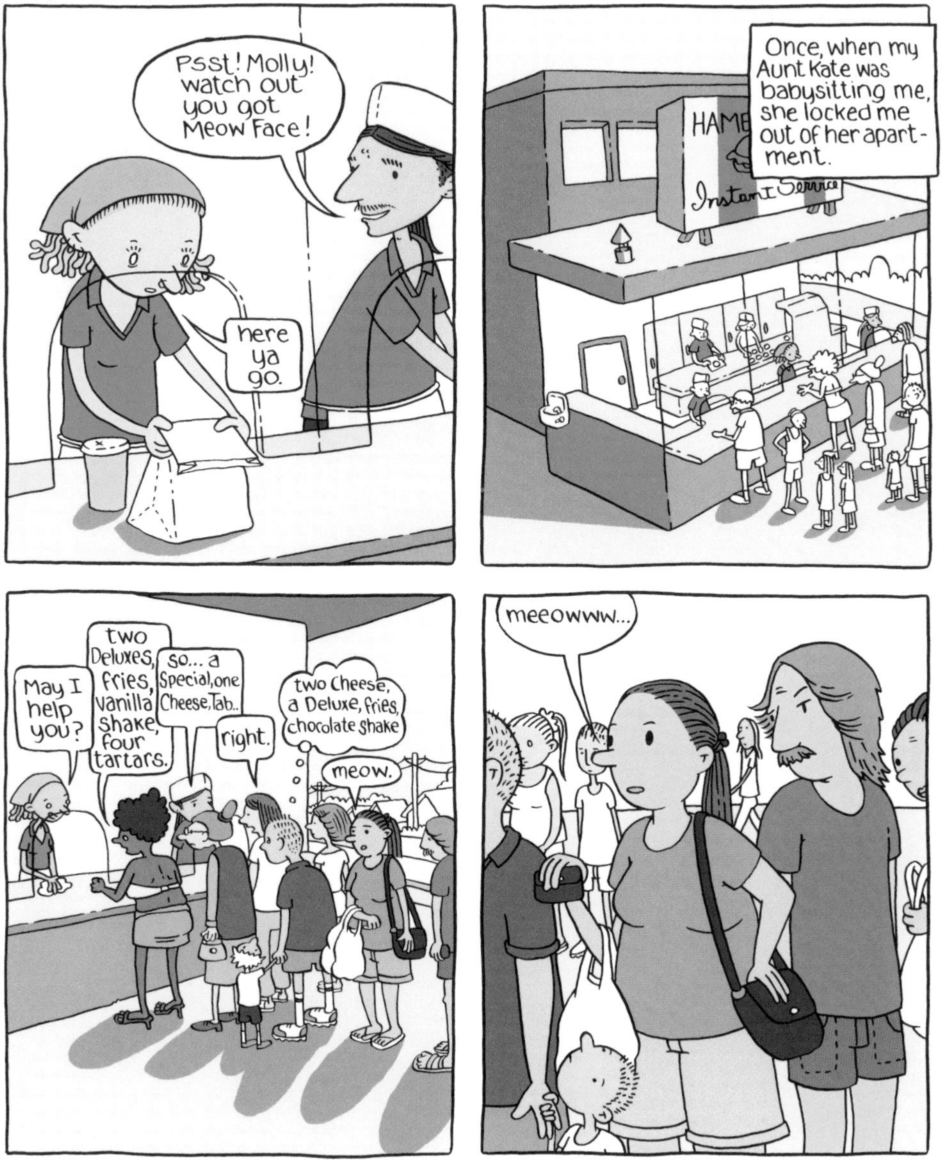

Psst! Molly! watch out you got Meow Face!
here ya go.
Once, when my Aunt Kate was babysitting me, she locked me out of her apartment.
HAMB
Instant Service
May I help you?
two Deluxes, fries, vanilla shake, four tartars.
so... a Special, one Cheese, Tab..
right.
two Cheese, a Deluxe, fries, chocolate shake
meow.
meeowww...

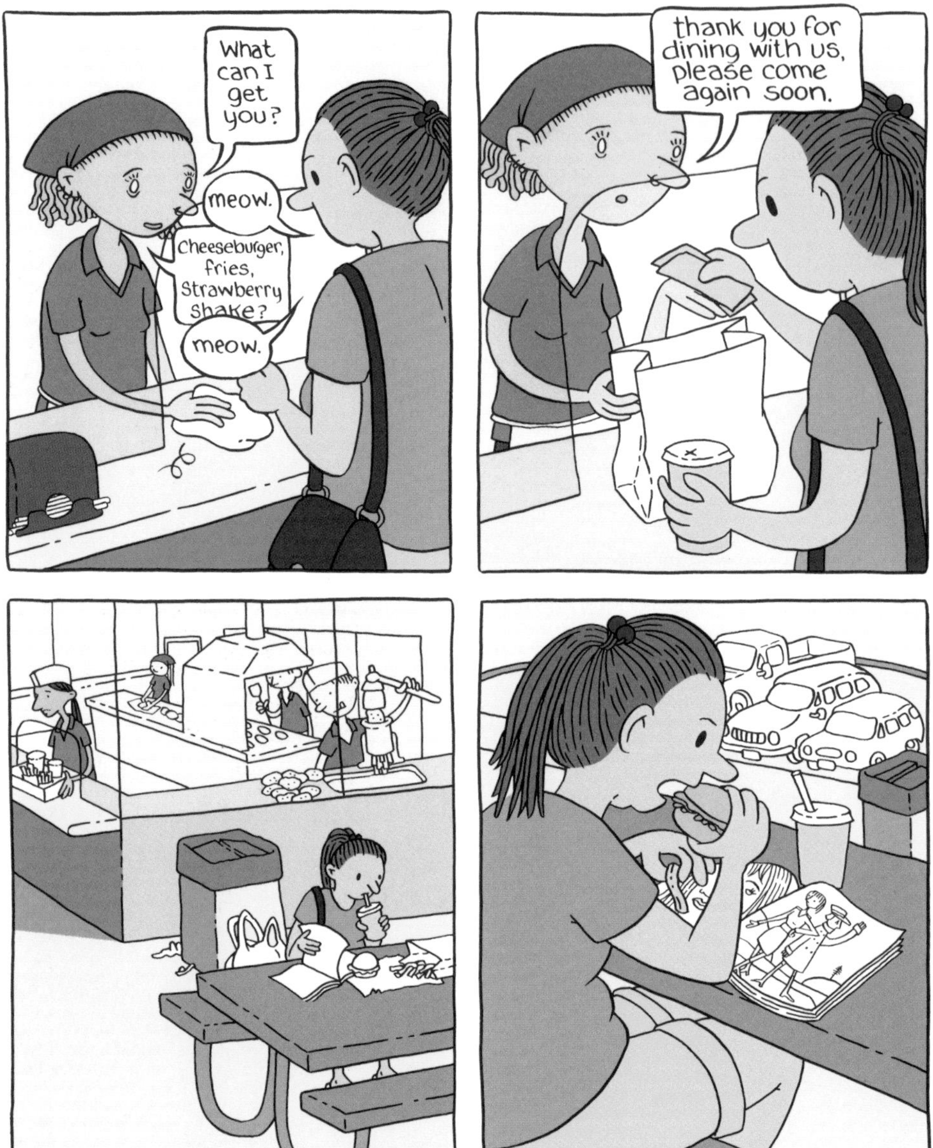
What can I get you?
meow.
Cheeseburger, fries, Strawberry shake?
meow.
thank you for dining with us, please come again soon.

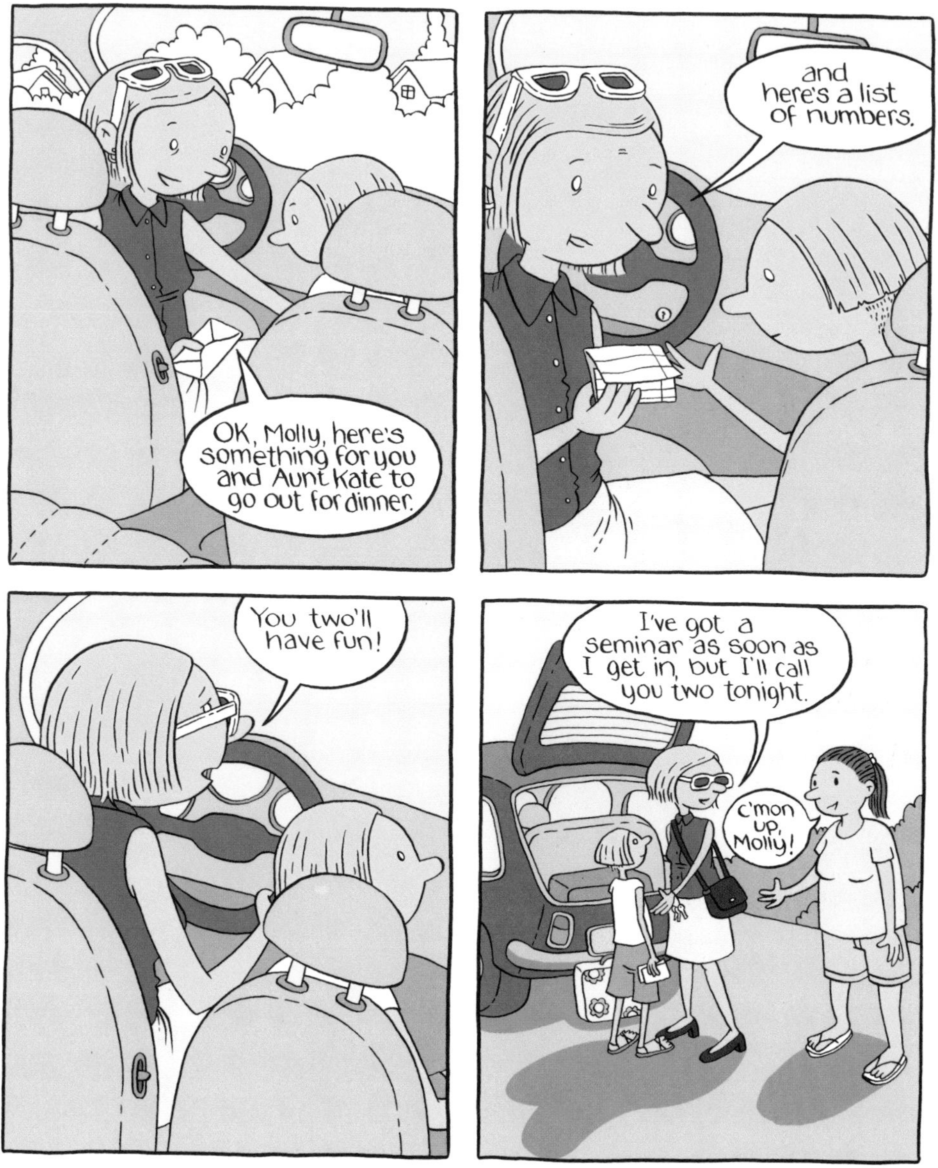
OK, Molly, here's something for you and Aunt Kate to go out for dinner.
and here's a list of numbers.
You two'll have fun!
I've got a seminar as soon as I get in, but I'll call you two tonight.
C'mon up, Molly!

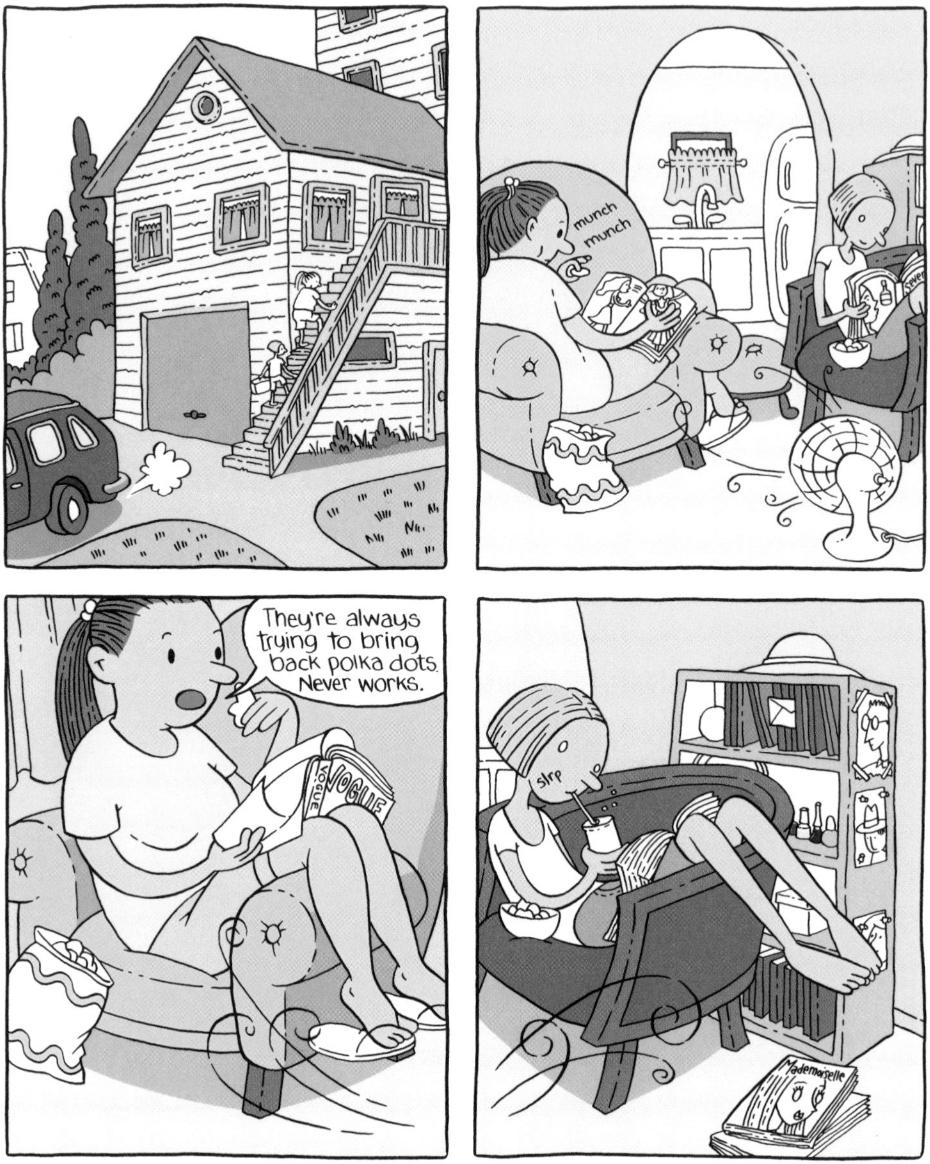
munch munch
They're always trying to bring back polka dots. Never works.
VOGUE
slrp
Mademoiselle

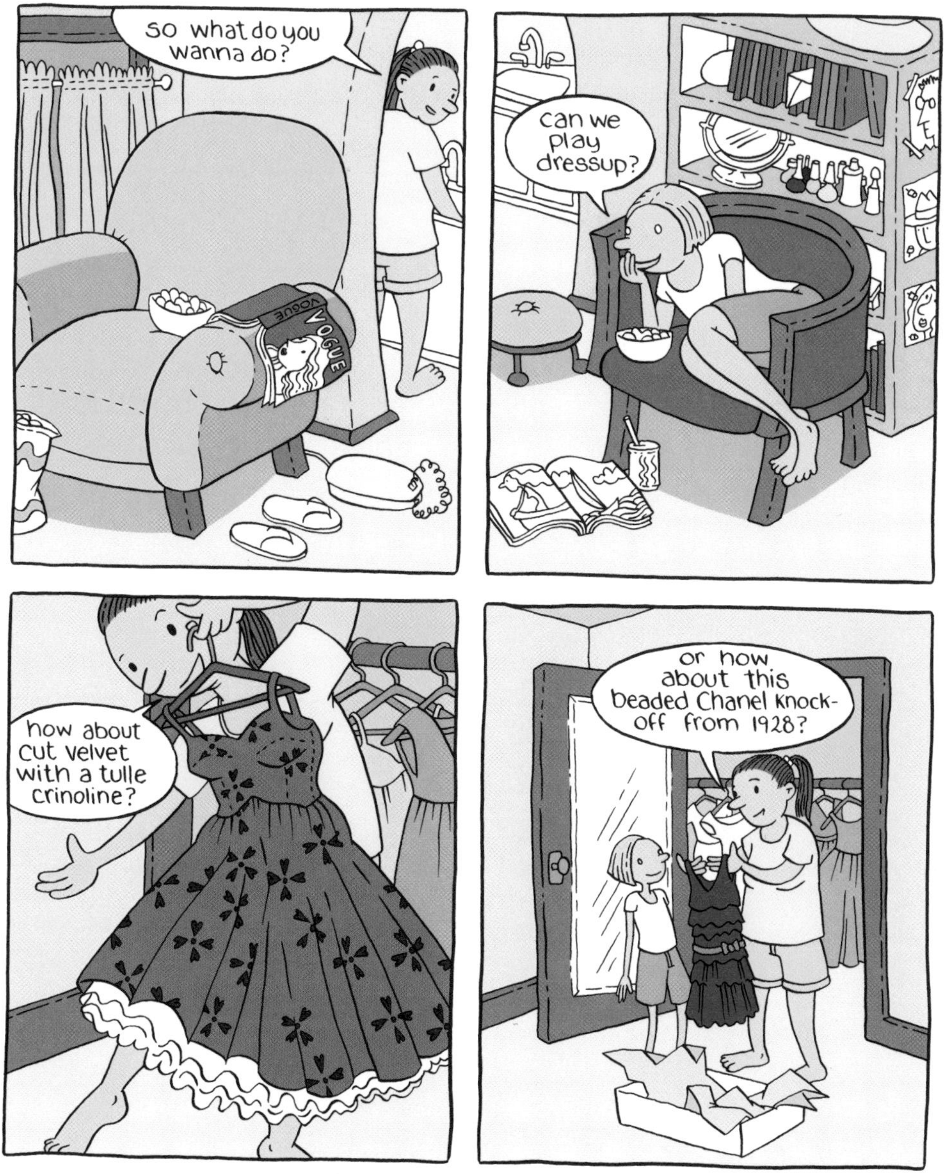
so what do you wanna do?
VOGUE
can we play dressup?
how about cut velvet with a tulle crinoline?
or how about this beaded Chanel knock-off from 1928?

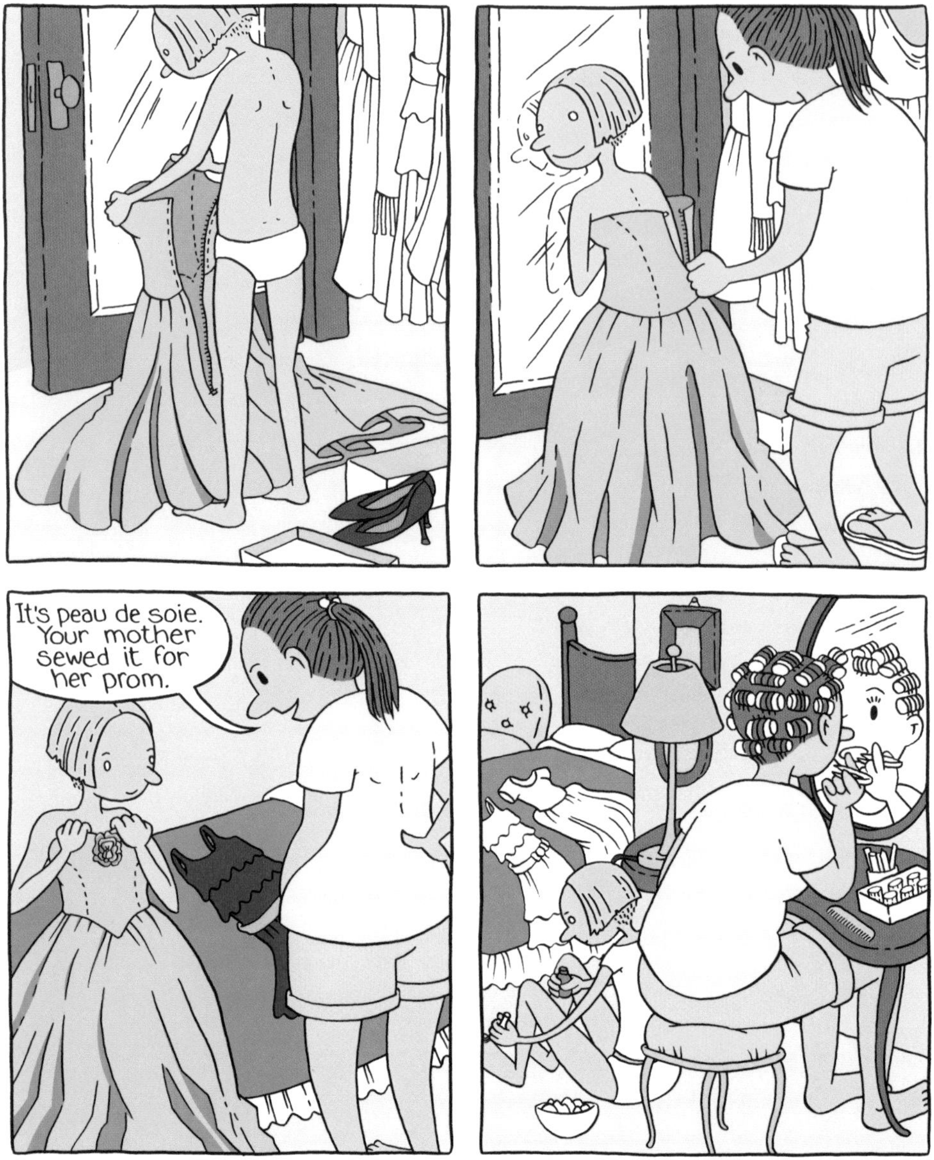
It's peau de soie. Your mother sewed it for her prom.

brrrng brrngg
brrnngg brrng br
fff
mmm-hmm... yep, first yer prom dress, now the green velvet-
vrrmmm
vrrrmm
vrm
vrrrmm
vrm
vrrrmm
Seventeen
vrmmm
vrmm
ez-blo
rrrmmmm
vrooomm
vroomm
vrooomm
hey Molly! ♪ta daaaa!♪

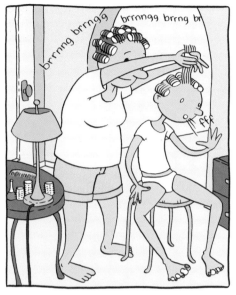

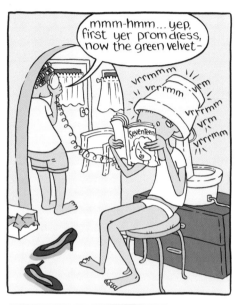

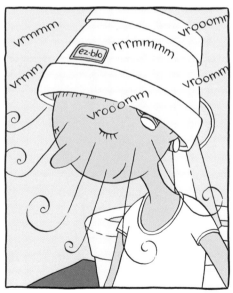

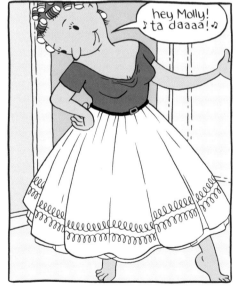

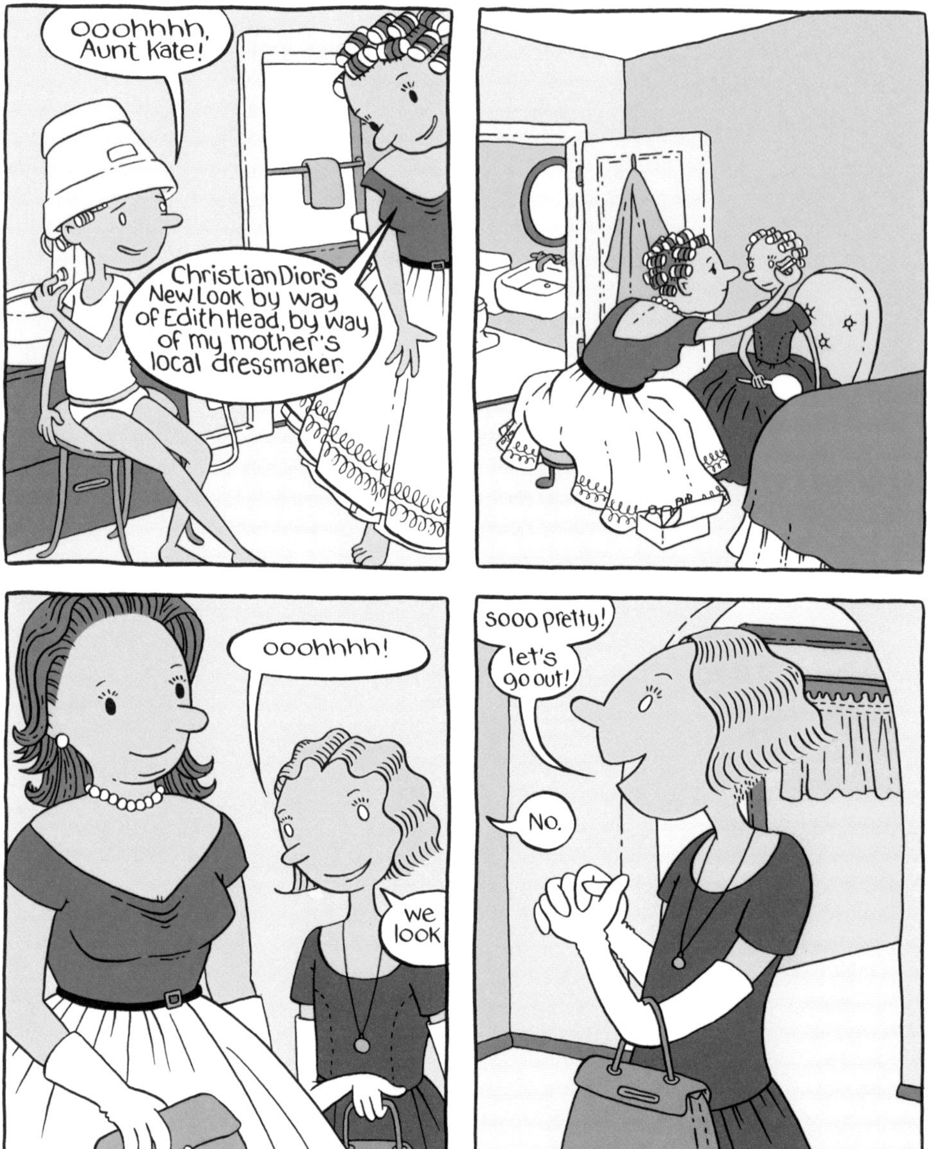
ooohhhh, Aunt Kate!
Christian Dior's New Look by way of Edith Head, by way of my mother's local dressmaker.
ooohhhh!
we look
sooo pretty!
let's go out!
No.

pleease?
no!
Aunt Kate, pleeease?
c'mon, it'll be funnn! We can go to the Italian Spaghetti House —maybe not with the gloves, but in our dresses! Mommy gave us money for a nice dinner—
no, Molly!
NO.
but—
NO!!
SLAM!

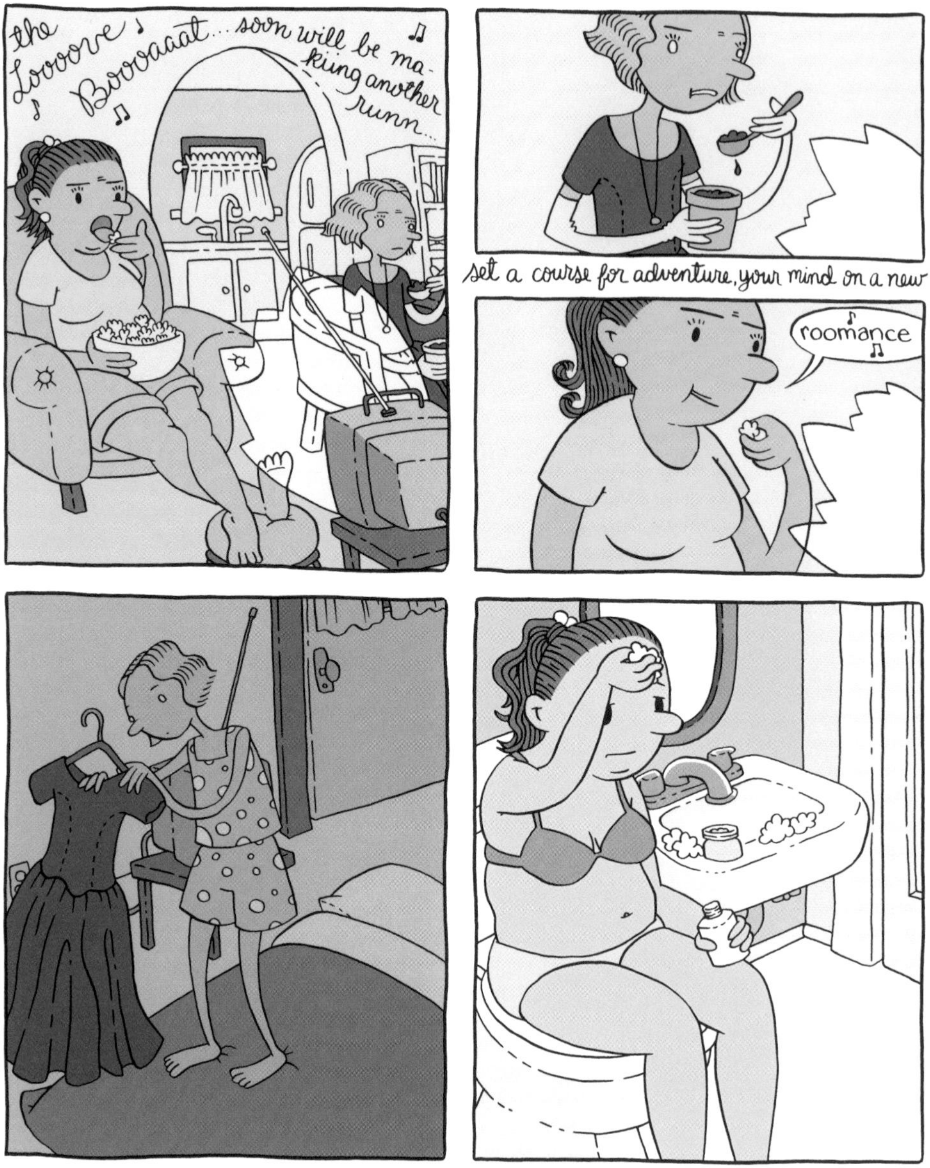
the Looooove Boooaaat... soon will be ma-king another runn...
set a course for adventure, your mind on a new
roomance

meow.......meowww
meoww.......meowowwwww......meeeoowwv

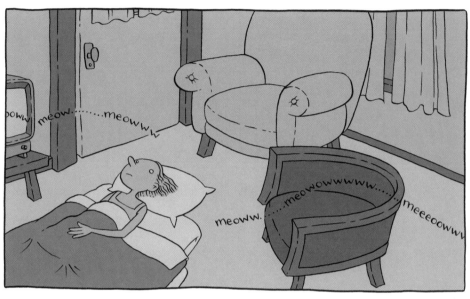

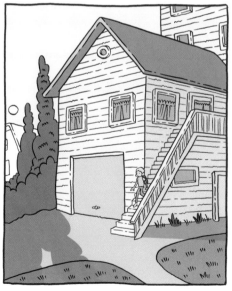

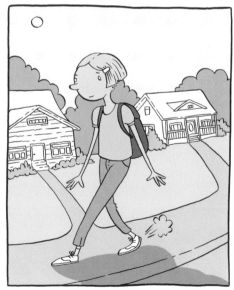

meow...
Respons
Cat Sit
chnk
chnk

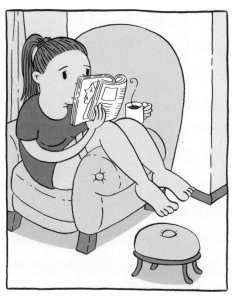

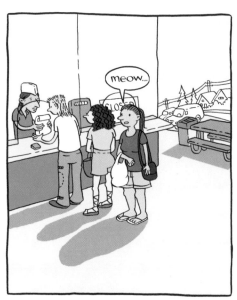

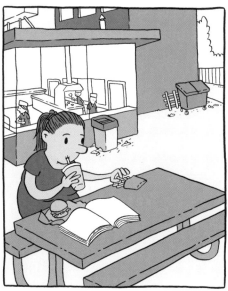

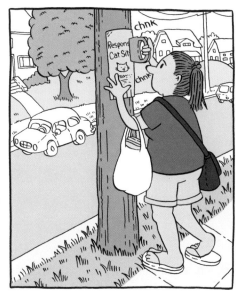

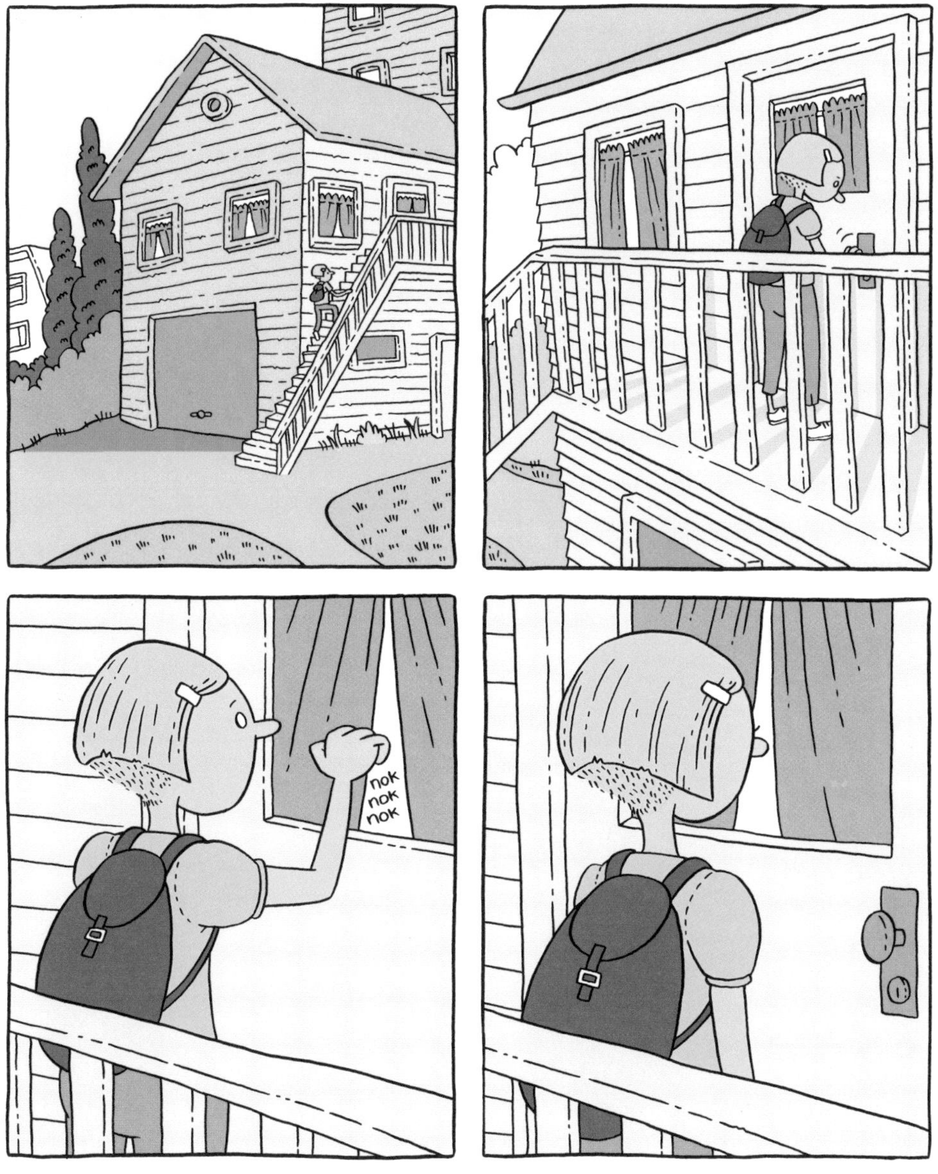
nok
nok
nok

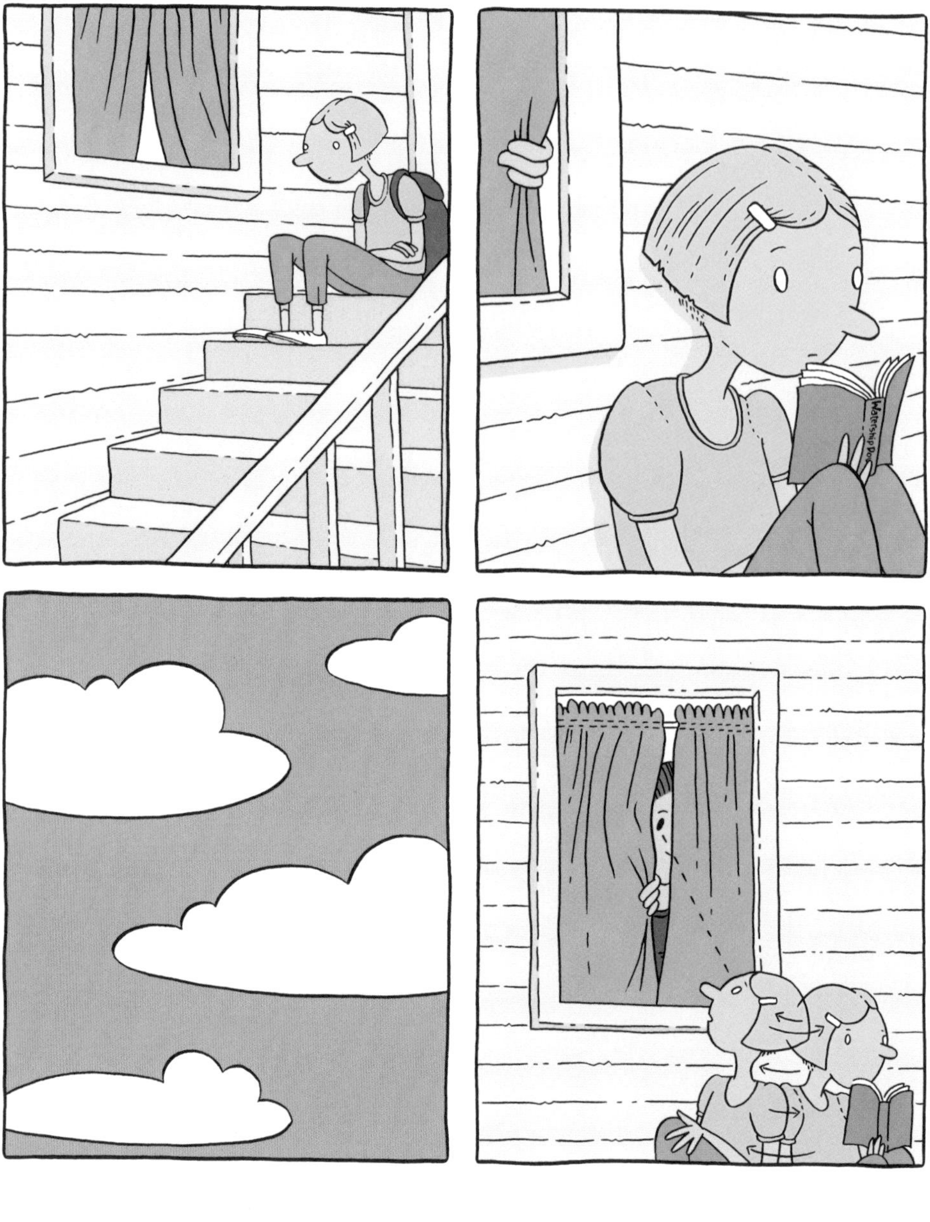
Watership Do

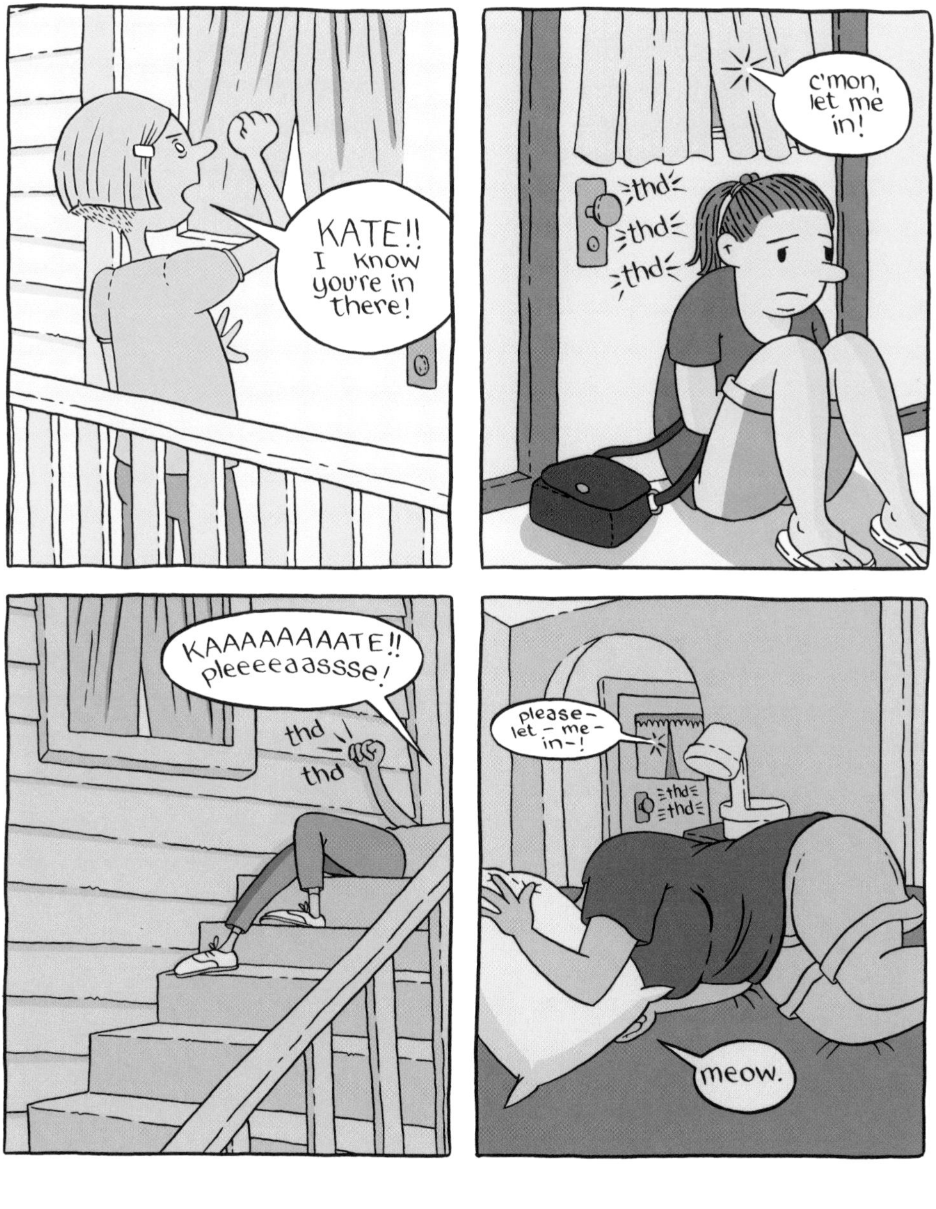
KATE!! I know you're in there!
c'mon, let me in!
thd
thd
thd
KAAAAAAAATE!! pleeeeaassse!
thd
thd
please- let - me - in-!
thd
thd
meow.

what can I get you?
a cheese-burger, fries, and a choc-olate shake.
that'll be three seventy two

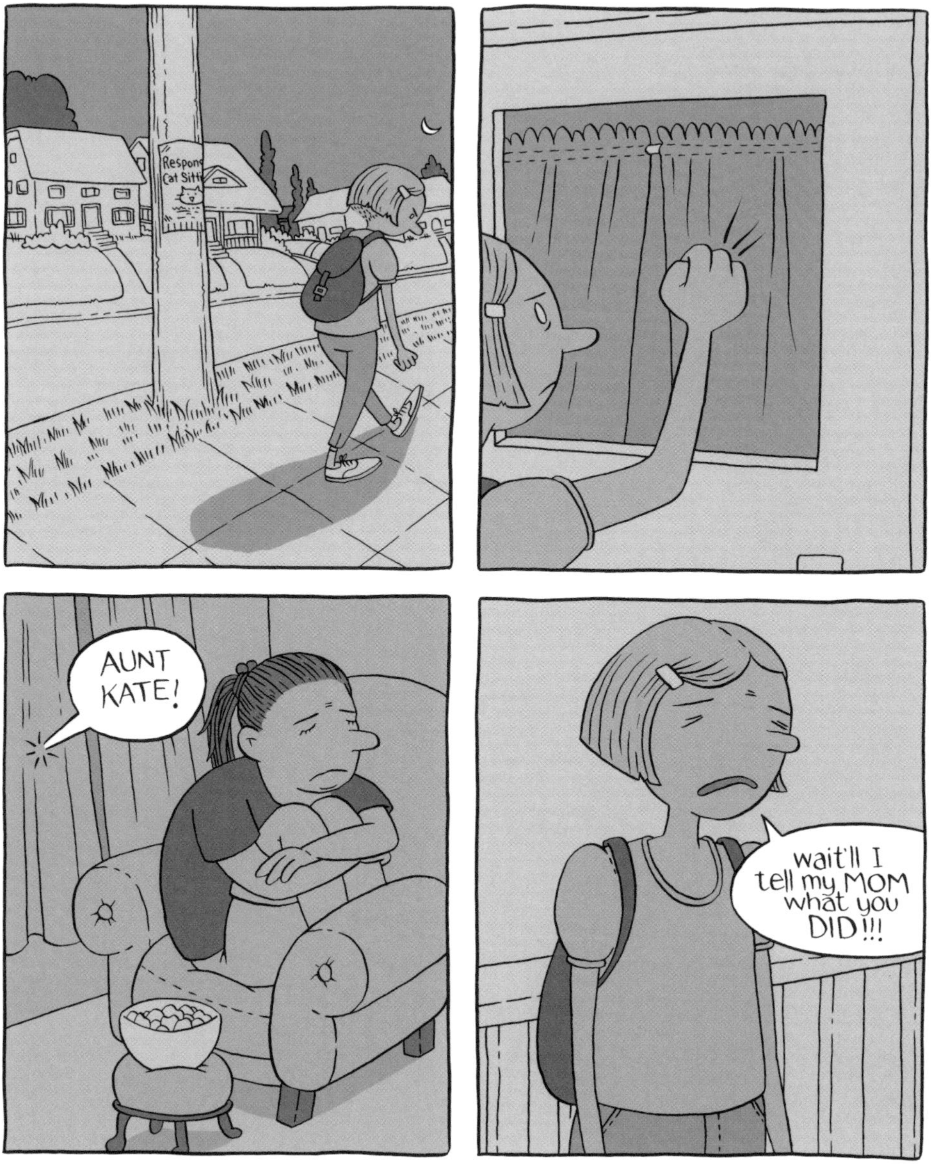
AUNT KATE!
wait'll I tell my MOM what you DID!!!

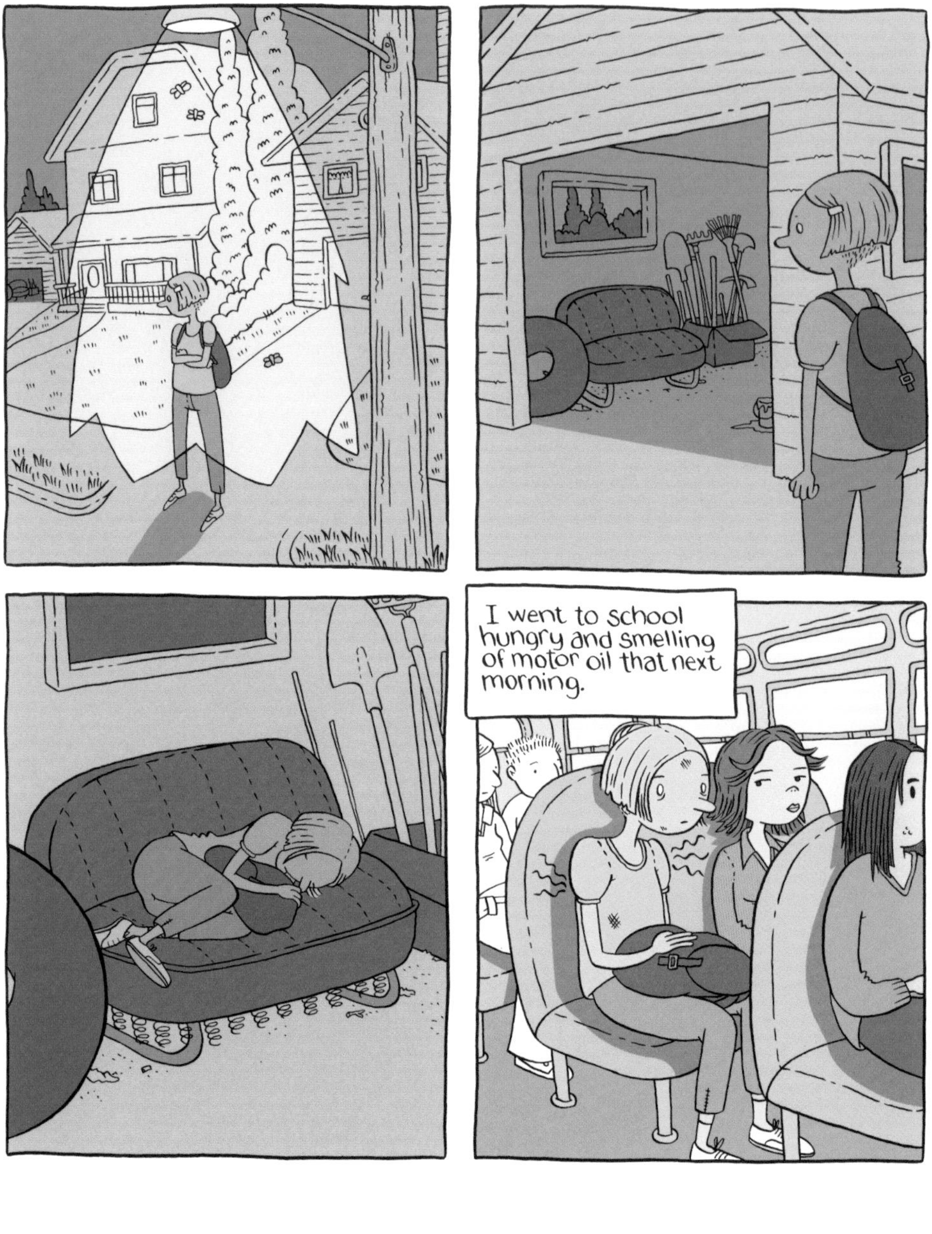
I went to school hungry and smelling of motor oil that next morning.

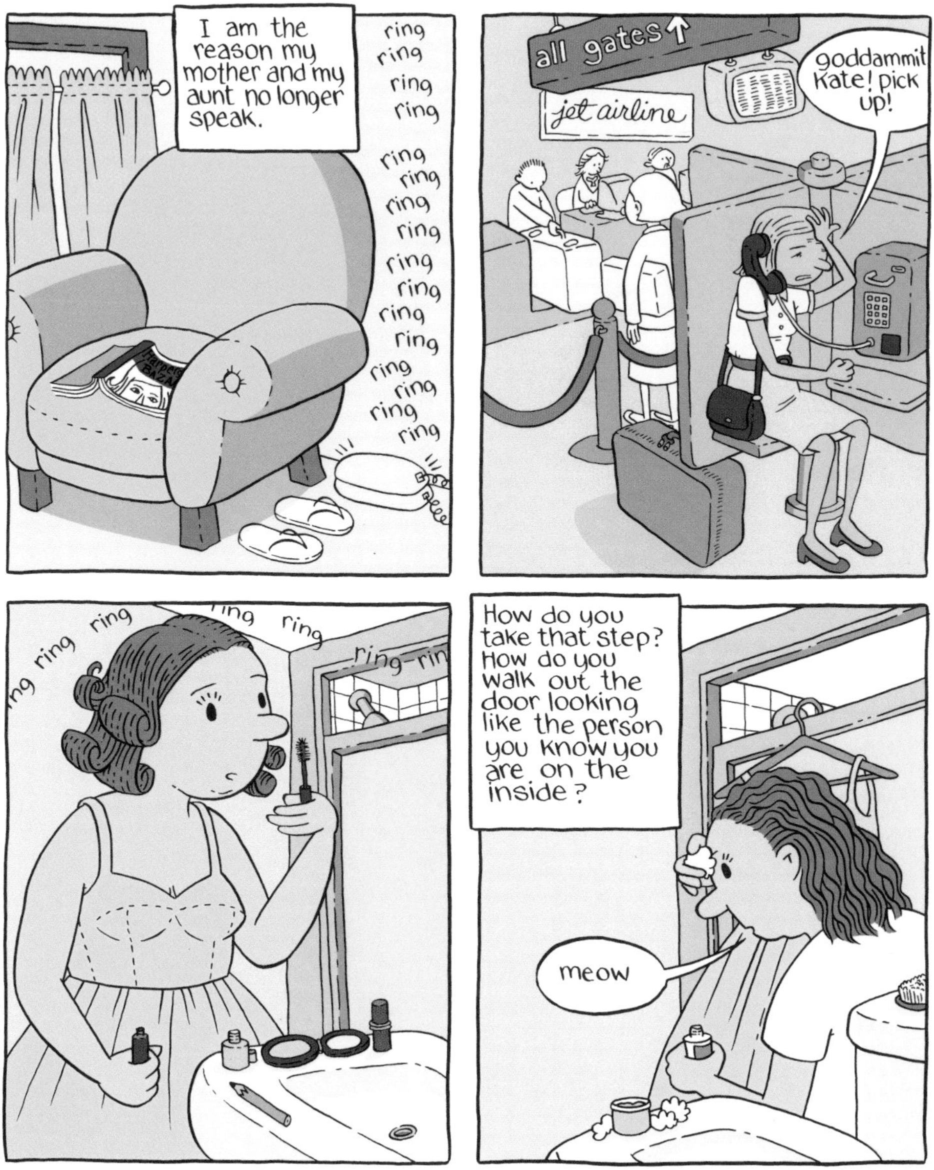
I am the reason my mother and my aunt no longer speak.
ring ring ring ring
ring ring ring ring ring ring ring ring ring ring ring ring
all gates
jet airline
goddammit Kate! pick up!
ring ring ring ring ring ring
How do you take that step? How do you walk out the door looking like the person you know you are on the inside?
meow

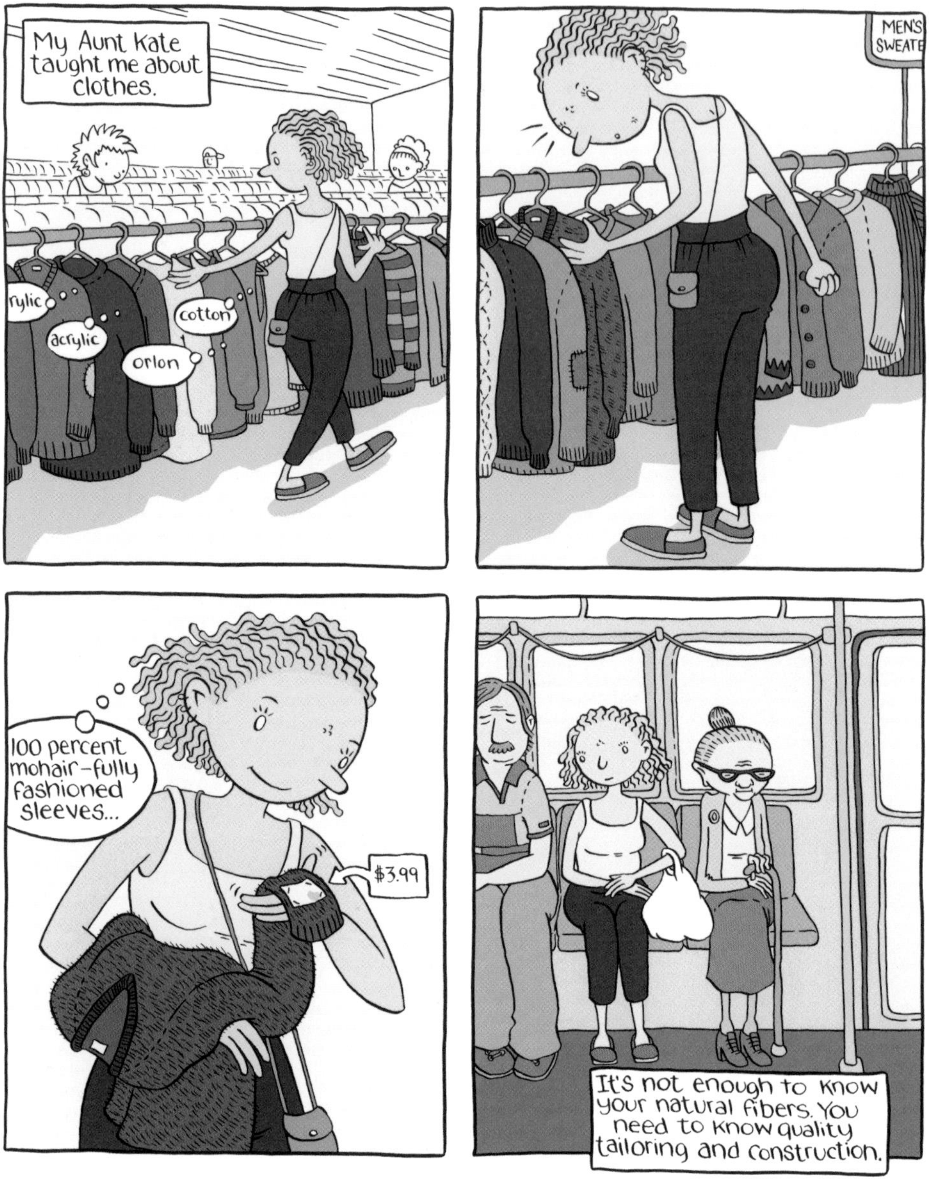
My Aunt Kate taught me about clothes.
rylic
acrylic
orlon
cotton
MEN'S SWEATE
100 percent mohair-fully fashioned sleeves...
$3.99
It's not enough to know your natural fibers. You need to know quality tailoring and construction.

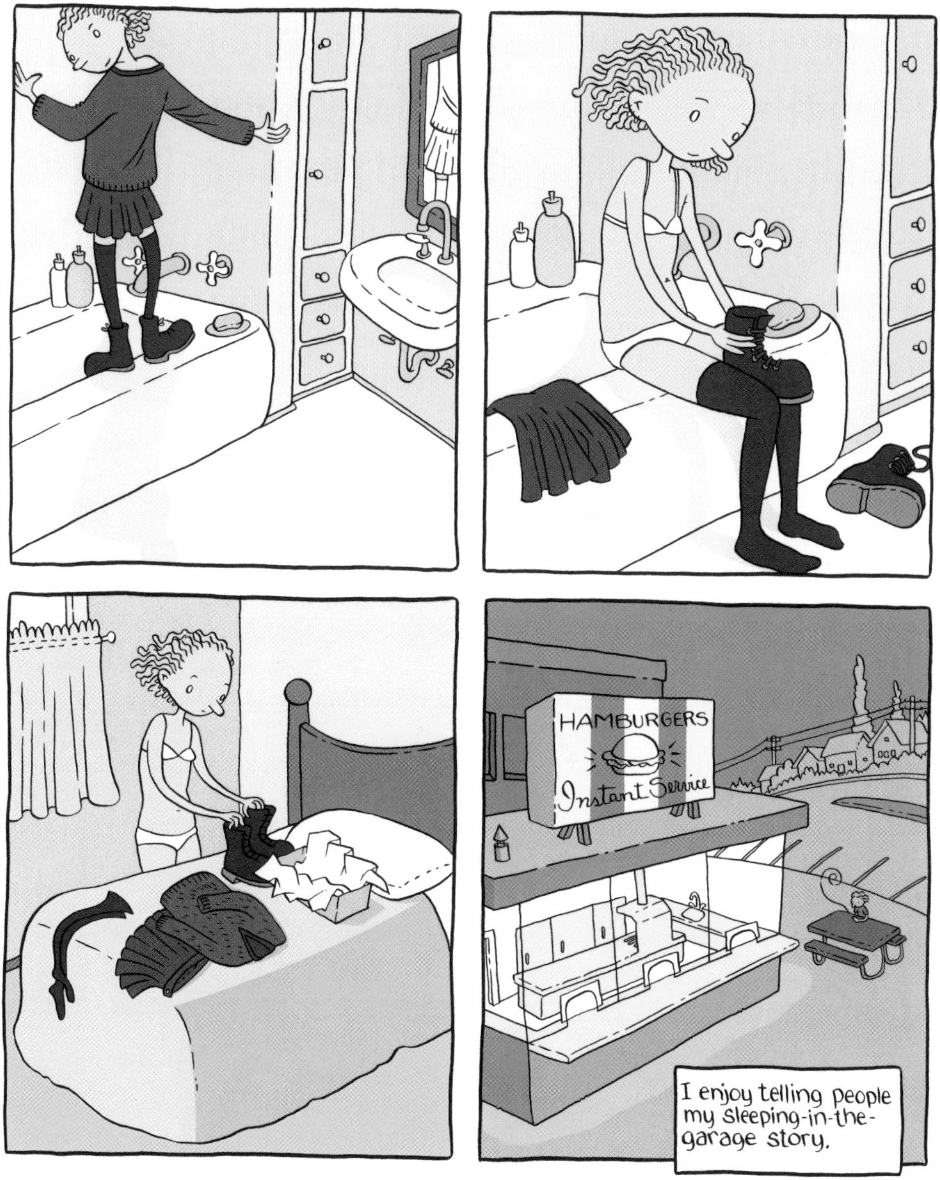
HAMBURGERS
Instant Service
I enjoy telling people my sleeping-in-the-garage story.

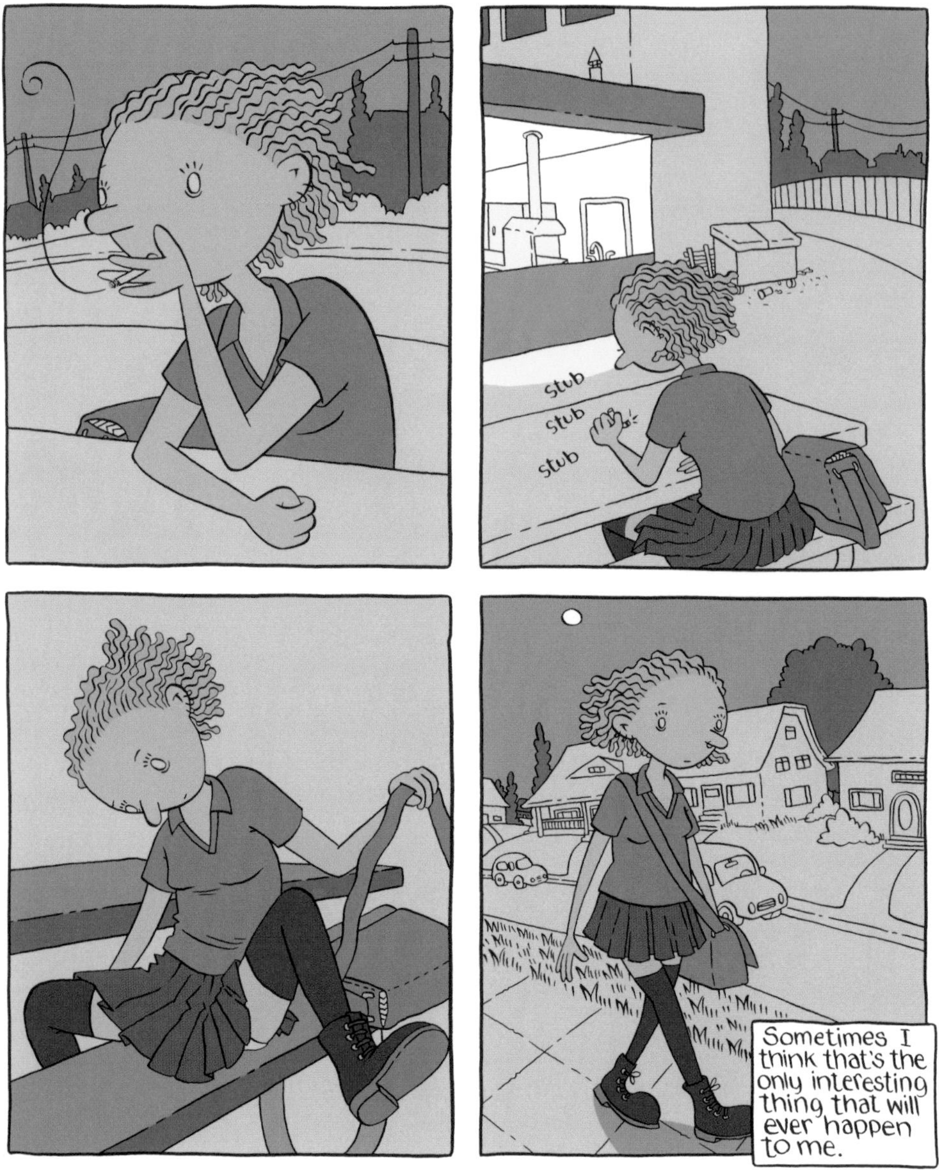
stub
stub
stub
Sometimes I think that's the only interesting thing that will ever happen to me.

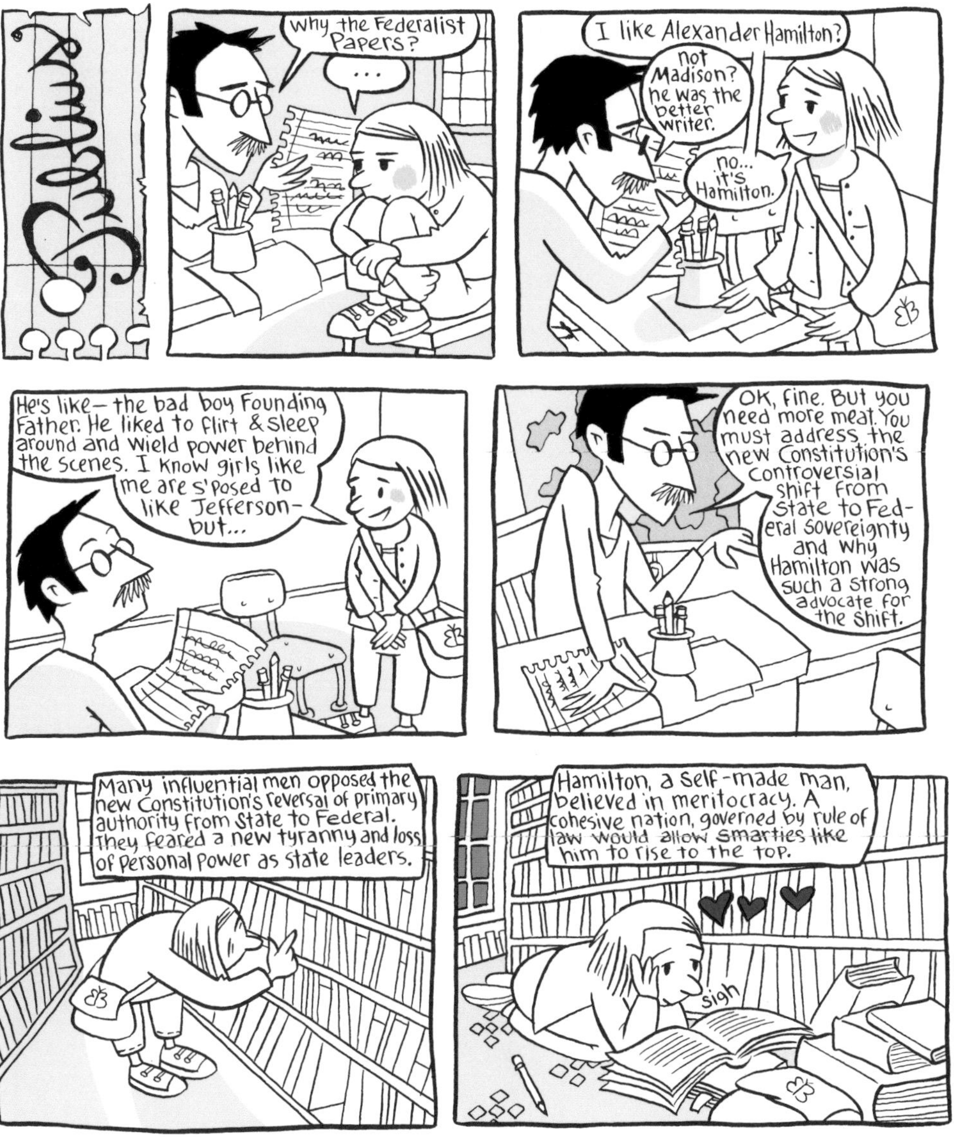
Smitten
why the Federalist Papers?
...
I like Alexander Hamilton?
not Madison? he was the better writer.
no... it's Hamilton.
He's like— the bad boy Founding Father. He liked to flirt & sleep around and wield power behind the scenes. I know girls like me are s'posed to like Jefferson— but...
OK, fine. But you need more meat. You must address the new Constitution's controversial shift from State to Federal sovereignty and why Hamilton was such a strong advocate for the shift.
Many influential men opposed the new Constitution's reversal of primary authority from State to Federal. They feared a new tyranny and loss of personal power as state leaders.
Hamilton, a self-made man, believed in meritocracy. A cohesive nation, governed by rule of law would allow Smarties like him to rise to the top.
sigh

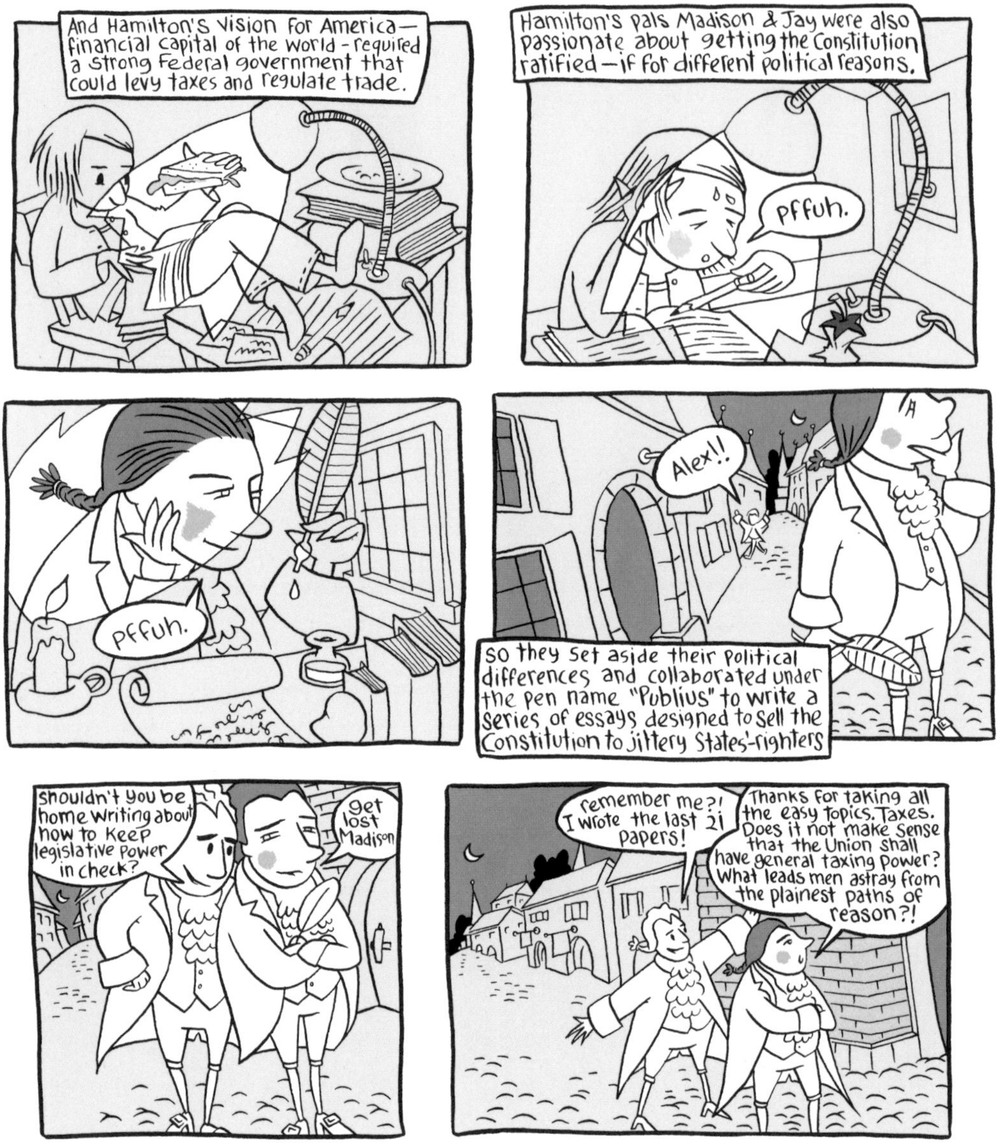
And Hamilton's vision for America— financial capital of the world - required a strong Federal government that could levy taxes and regulate trade.
Hamilton's pals Madison & Jay were also passionate about getting the Constitution ratified—if for different political reasons.
pffuh.
pffuh.
Alex!!
So they set aside their political differences and collaborated under the pen name "Publius" to write a series of essays designed to sell the Constitution to jittery States'-righters
Shouldn't you be home writing about how to keep legislative power in check?
get lost Madison
remember me?! I wrote the last 21 papers!
Thanks for taking all the easy topics. Taxes. Does it not make sense that the Union shall have general taxing power? What leads men astray from the plainest paths of reason?!

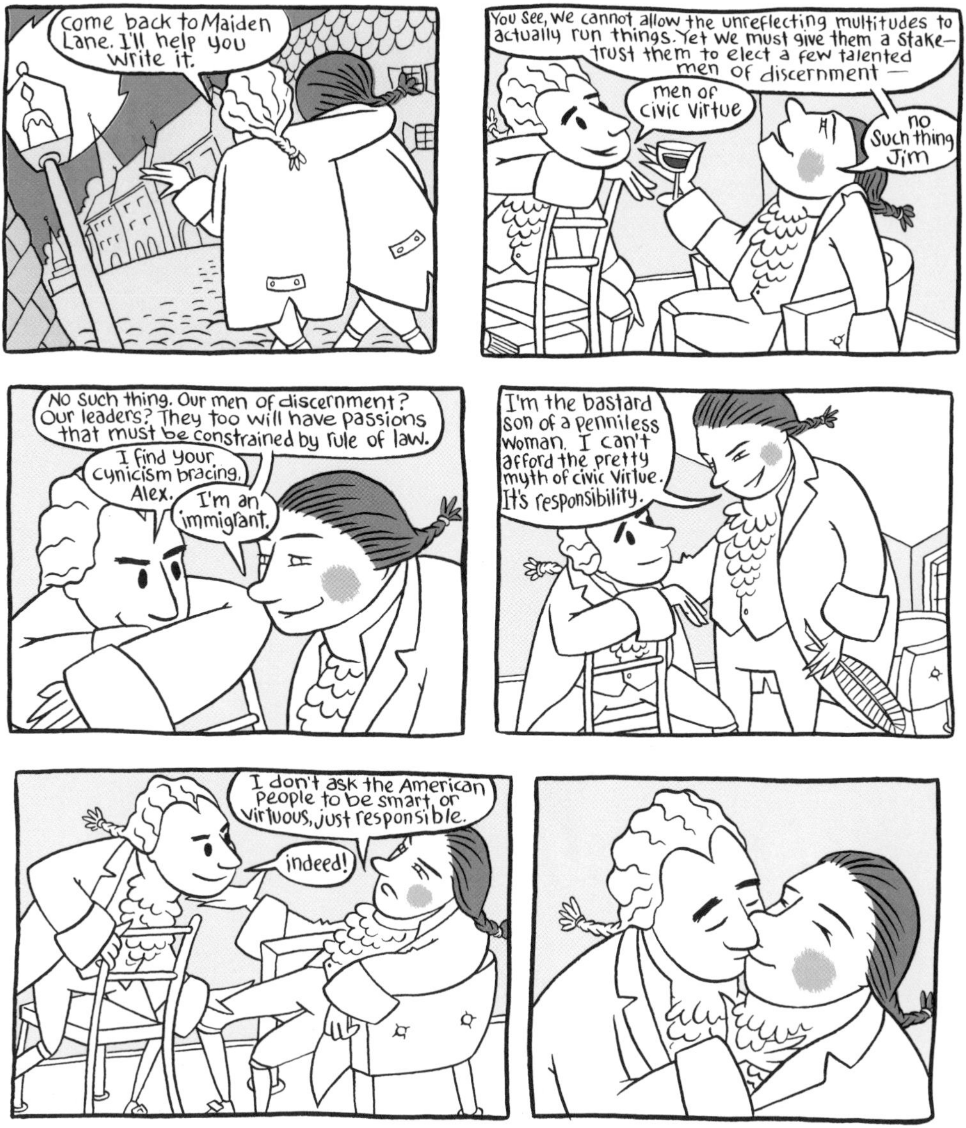
Come back to Maiden Lane. I'll help you write it.
You see, we cannot allow the unreflecting multitudes to actually run things. Yet we must give them a stake— trust them to elect a few talented men of discernment—
men of civic virtue
no such thing Jim
No such thing. Our men of discernment? Our leaders? They too will have passions that must be constrained by rule of law.
I find your cynicism bracing, Alex.
I'm an immigrant.
I'm the bastard son of a penniless woman. I can't afford the pretty myth of civic virtue. It's responsibility.
I don't ask the American people to be smart, or virtuous, just responsible.
indeed!

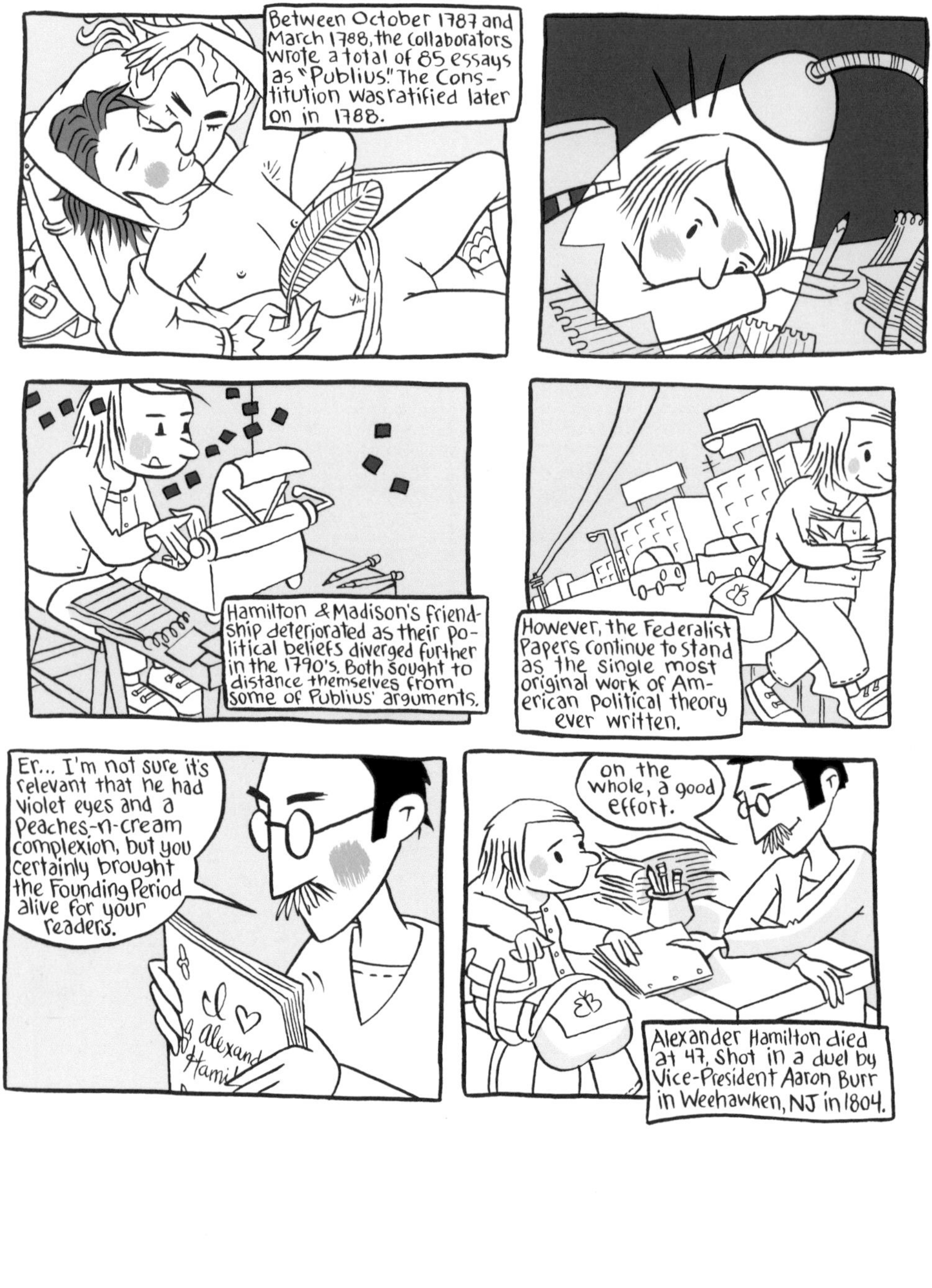
Between October 1787 and March 1788, the collaborators wrote a total of 85 essays as "Publius." The Constitution was ratified later on in 1788.
Hamilton & Madison's friendship deteriorated as their political beliefs diverged further in the 1790's. Both sought to distance themselves from some of Publius' arguments.
However, the Federalist Papers continue to stand as the single most original work of American political theory ever written.
Er... I'm not sure it's relevant that he had violet eyes and a peaches-n-cream complexion, but you certainly brought the Founding Period alive for your readers.
on the whole, a good effort.
Alexander Hamilton died at 47, shot in a duel by Vice-President Aaron Burr in Weehawken, NJ in 1804.

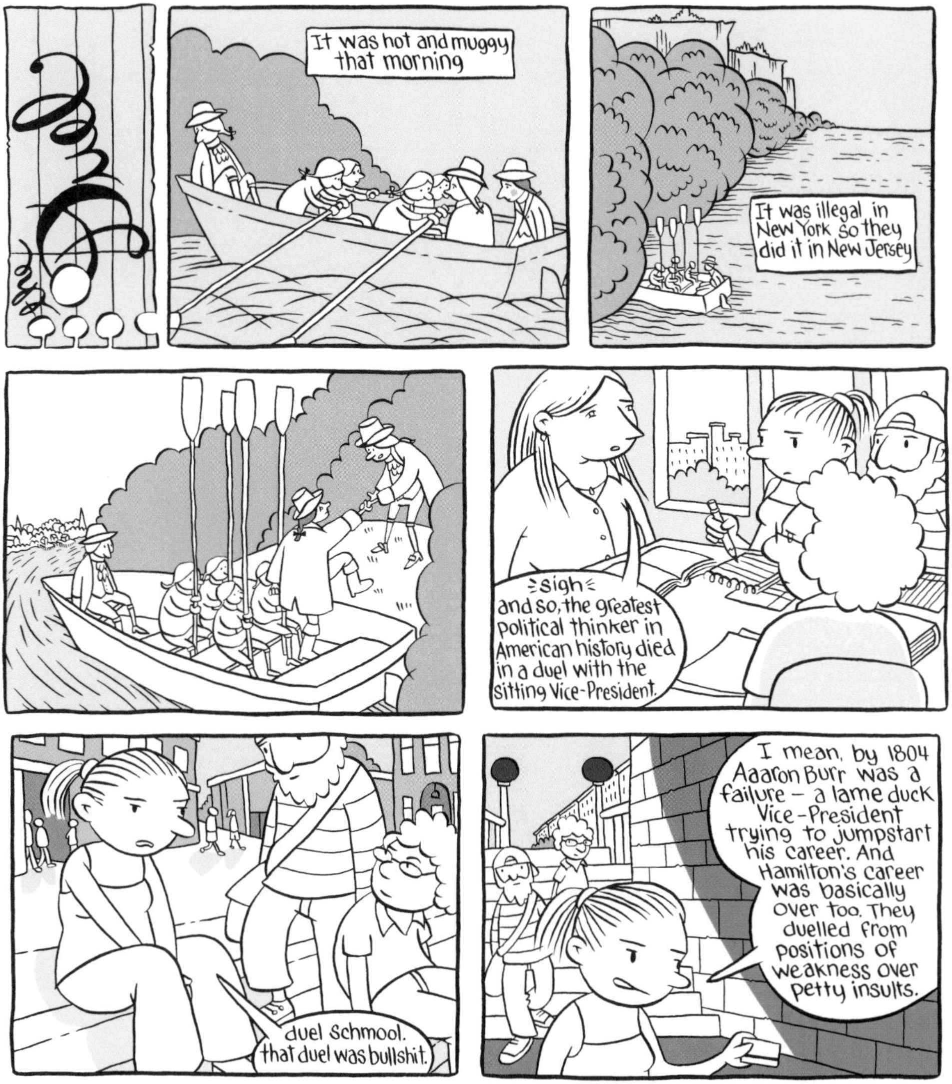
It was hot and muggy that morning
It was illegal in New York so they did it in New Jersey
sigh
and so, the greatest political thinker in American history died in a duel with the sitting Vice-President.
duel schmool. that duel was bullshit.
I mean, by 1804 Aaaron Burr was a failure – a lame duck Vice-President trying to jumpstart his career. And Hamilton's career was basically over too. They duelled from positions of weakness over petty insults.

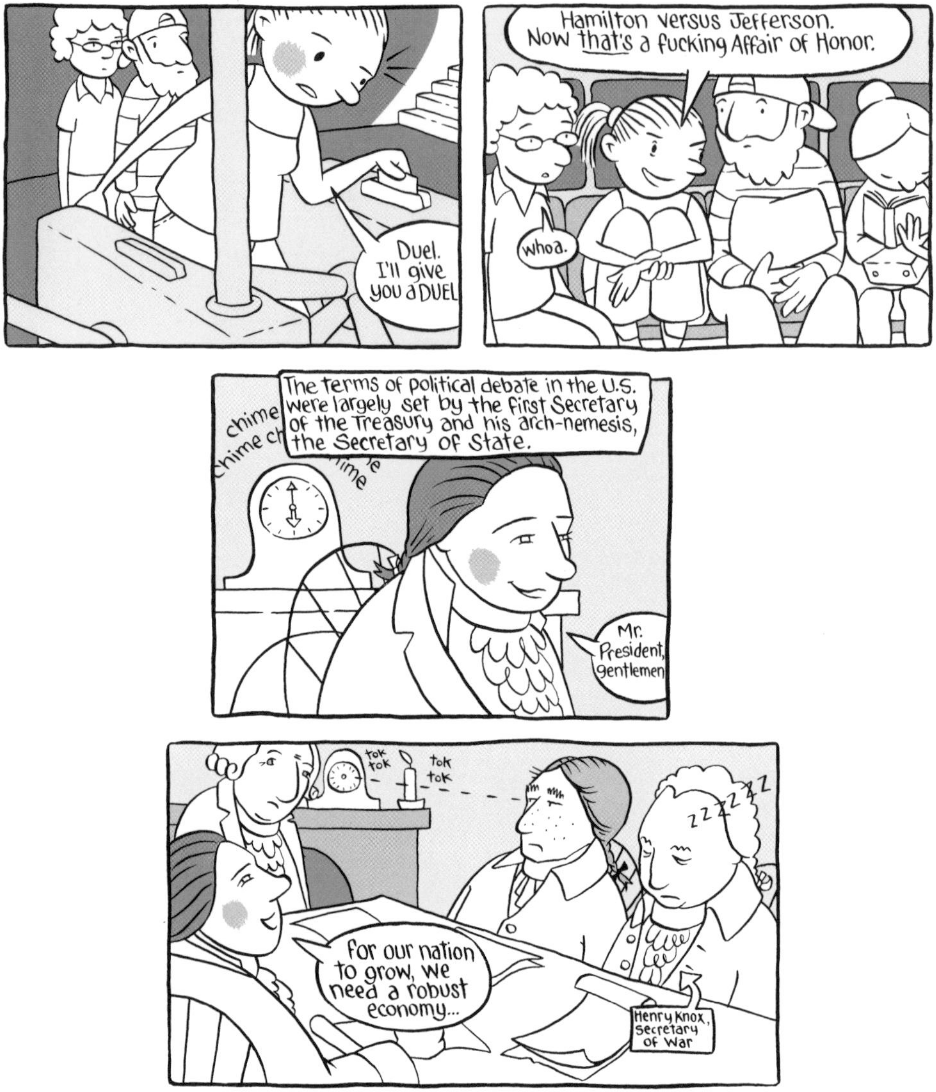
Duel. I'll give you a DUEL
Hamilton versus Jefferson. Now that's a fucking Affair of Honor.
whoa.
The terms of political debate in the U.S. were largely set by the first Secretary of the Treasury and his arch-nemesis, the Secretary of State.
chime
Mr. President, gentlemen
tok tok
tok tok
zzzzzzz
for our nation to grow, we need a robust economy...
Henry Knox, Secretary of War

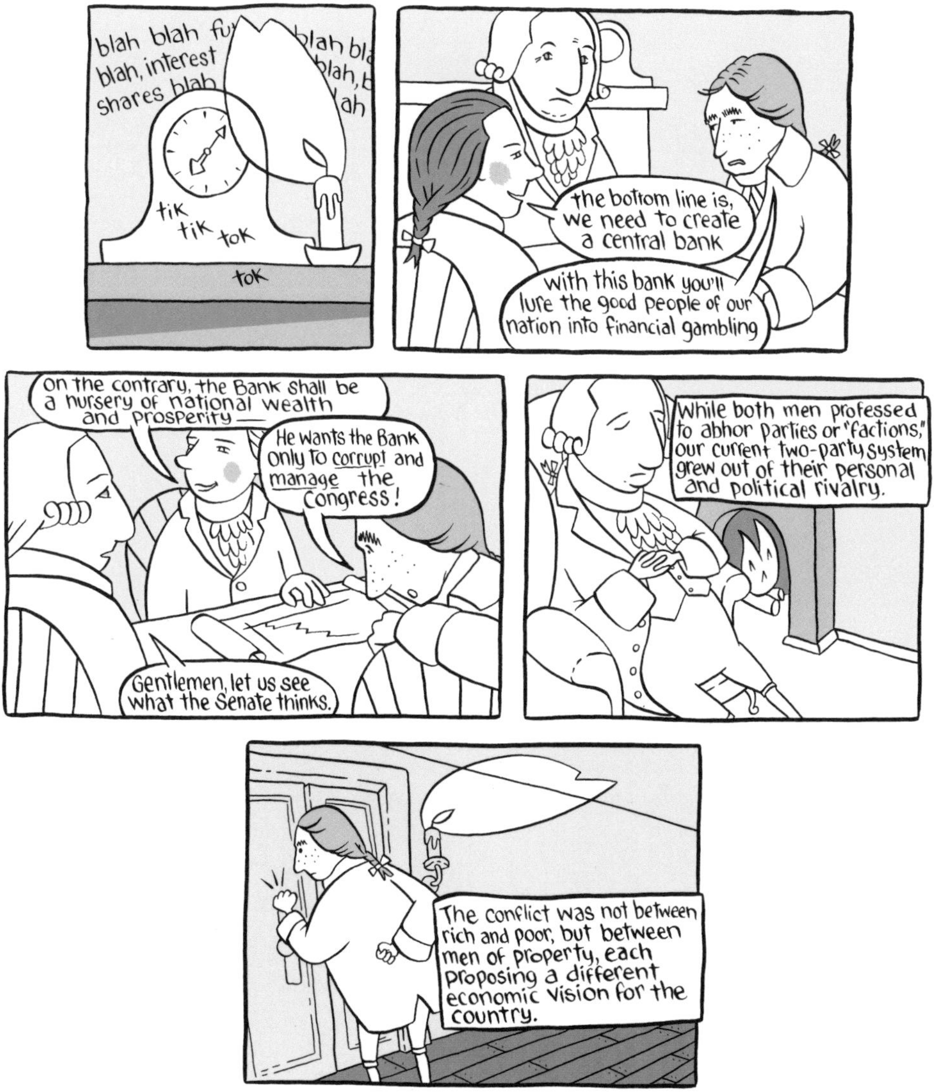
blah blah fu
blah, interest
shares blah
blah bl
blah, b
ah
tik
tik
tok
tok
the bottom line is, we need to create a central bank
with this bank you'll lure the good people of our nation into financial gambling
On the contrary, the Bank shall be a nursery of national wealth and prosperity —
He wants the Bank only to corrupt and manage the Congress!
Gentlemen, let us see what the Senate thinks.
While both men professed to abhor parties or "factions," our current two-party system grew out of their personal and political rivalry.
The conflict was not between rich and poor, but between men of property, each proposing a different economic vision for the country.

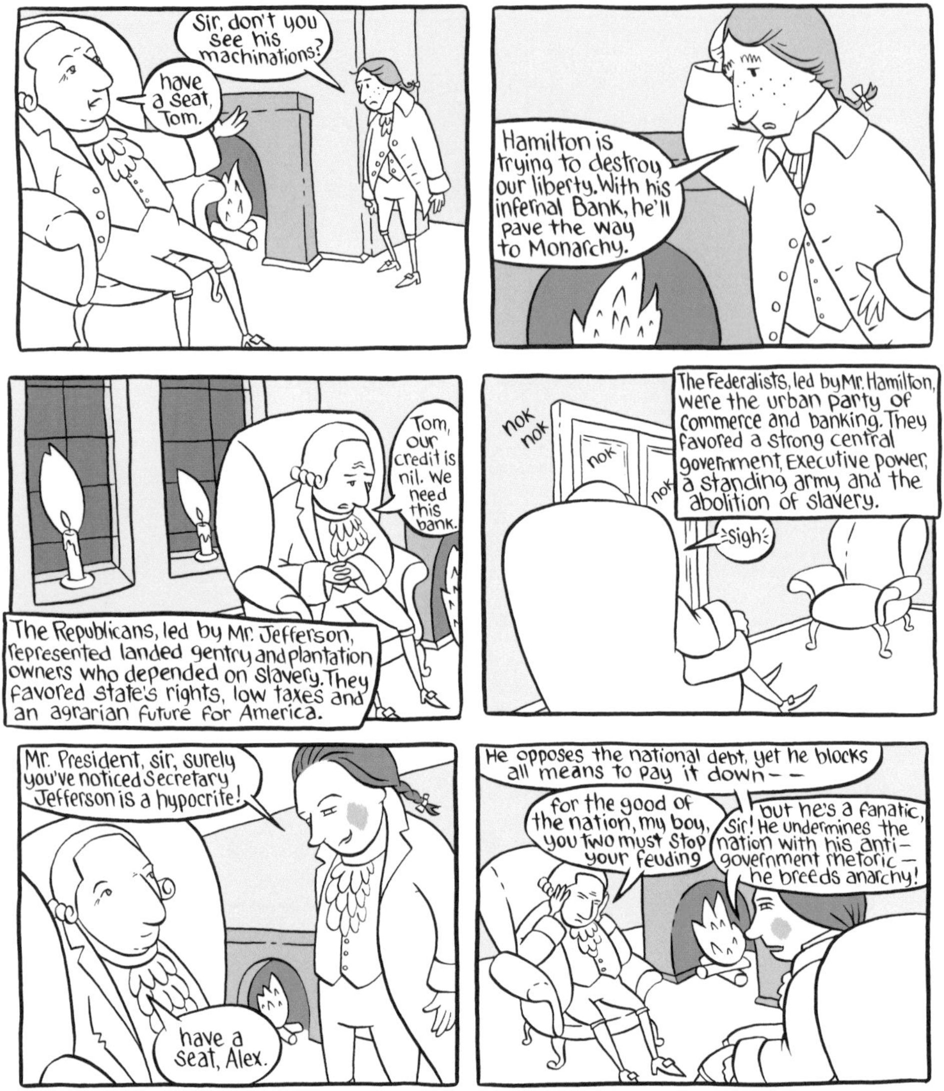
Sir, don't you see his machinations?
have a seat, Tom.
Hamilton is trying to destroy our liberty. With his infernal Bank, he'll pave the way to Monarchy.
Tom, our credit is nil. We need this bank.
The Republicans, led by Mr. Jefferson, represented landed gentry and plantation owners who depended on slavery. They favored state's rights, low taxes and an agrarian future for America.
nok nok
nok
nok
The Federalists, led by Mr. Hamilton, were the urban party of commerce and banking. They favored a strong central government, Executive power, a standing army and the abolition of slavery.
Sigh
Mr. President, sir, surely you've noticed Secretary Jefferson is a hypocrite!
have a seat, Alex.
He opposes the national debt, yet he blocks all means to pay it down--
for the good of the nation, my boy, you two must stop your feuding
but he's a fanatic, Sir! He undermines the nation with his anti-government rhetoric— he breeds anarchy!

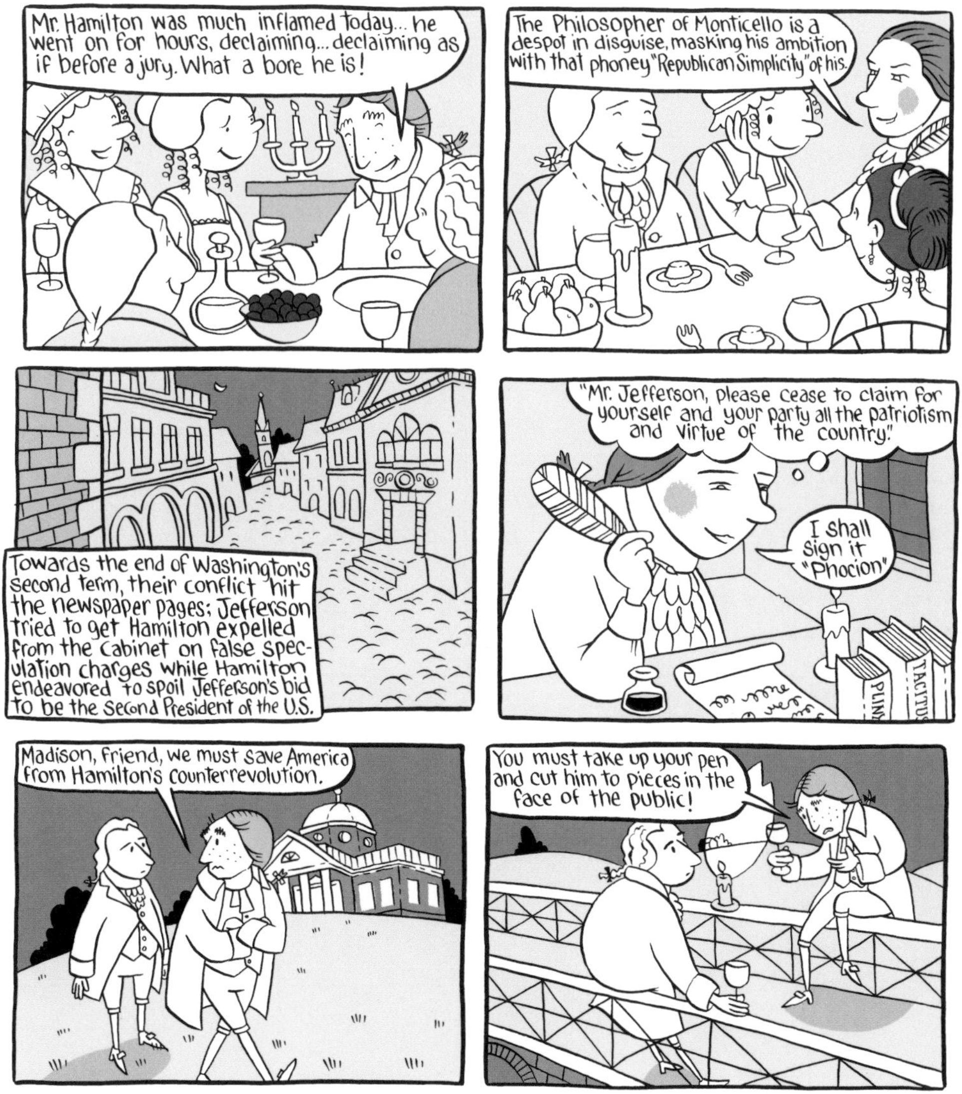

Mr. Hamilton was much inflamed today... he went on for hours, declaiming... declaiming as if before a jury. What a bore he is!
The Philosopher of Monticello is a despot in disguise, masking his ambition with that phoney "Republican Simplicity" of his.
Towards the end of Washington's second term, their conflict hit the newspaper pages; Jefferson tried to get Hamilton expelled from the Cabinet on false speculation charges while Hamilton endeavored to spoil Jefferson's bid to be the second President of the U.S.
"Mr. Jefferson, please cease to claim for yourself and your party all the patriotism and virtue of the country."
I shall sign it "Phocion"
PLINY
TACITUS
Madison, friend, we must save America from Hamilton's counterrevolution.
You must take up your pen and cut him to pieces in the face of the public!

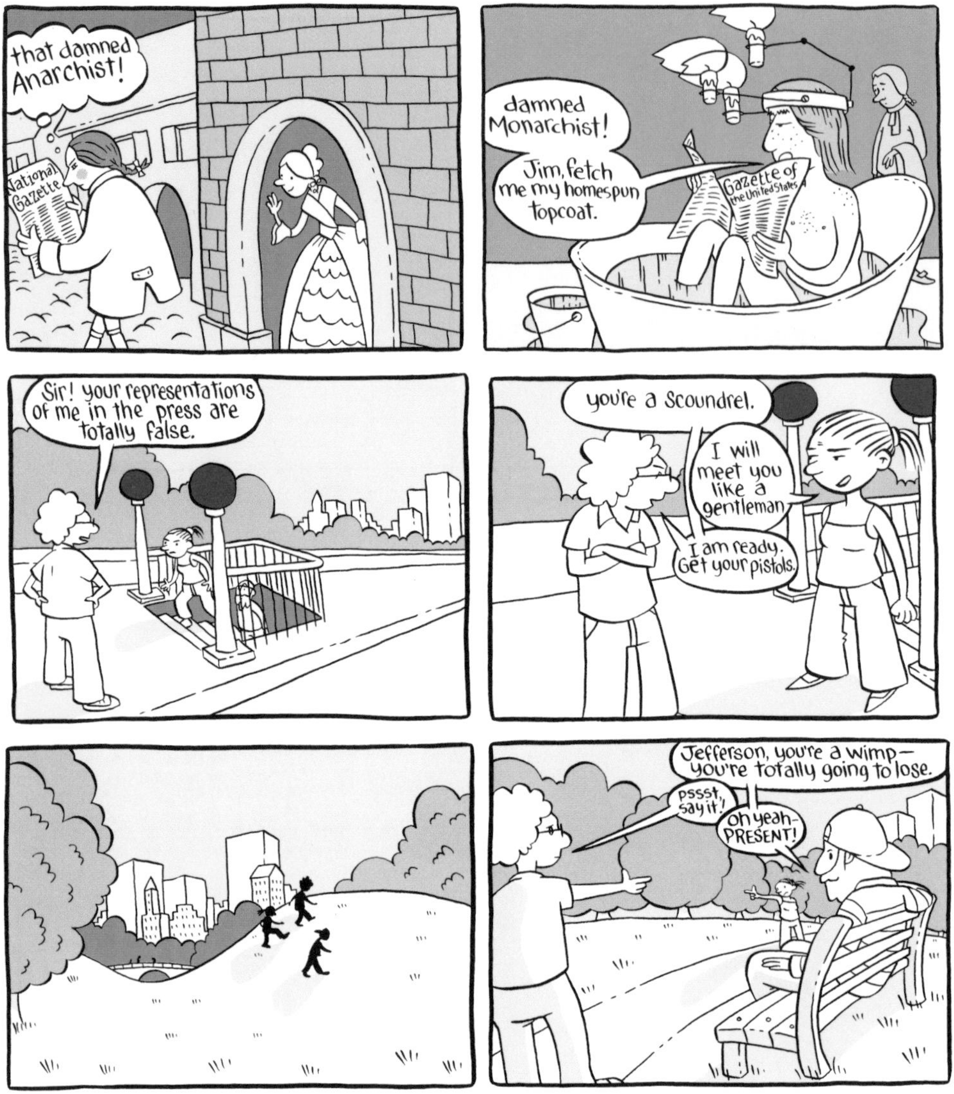
that damned Anarchist!
National Gazette
damned Monarchist!
Jim, fetch me my homespun topcoat.
Gazette of the United States
Sir! your representations of me in the press are totally false.
you're a Scoundrel.
I will meet you like a gentleman.
I am ready. Get your pistols.
Jefferson, you're a wimp— you're totally going to lose.
pssst, say it!
oh yeah- PRESENT!

For those of us who chafe at the unfairness of historical reputation, it is sweet to contemplate Hamilton victorious over Jefferson on the Field of Honor.

But that duel never happened. Instead they remain forever opposed, pistols cocked, aiming for each other's heads and we the people forever suspended between them.

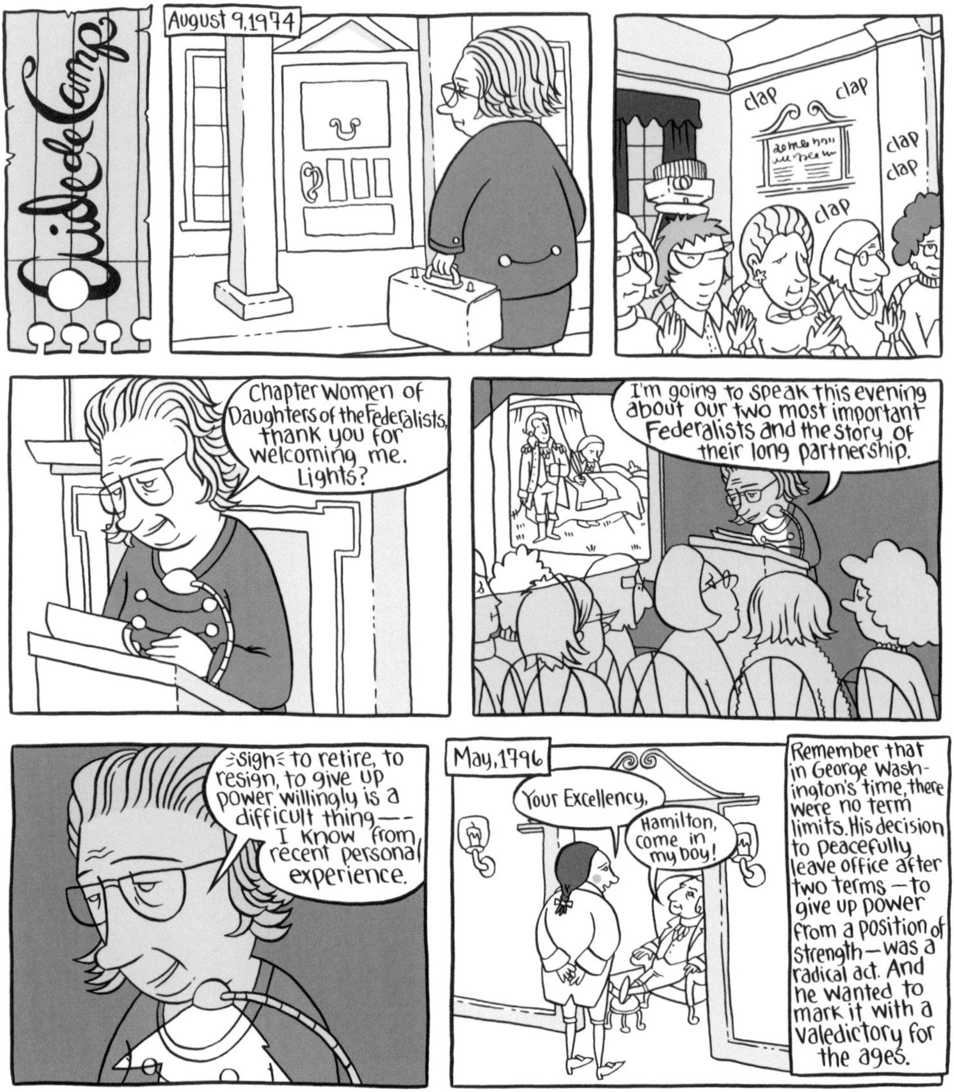
Aide de Camp
August 9, 1974
clap
clap
clap
clap
clap
Chapter Women of Daughters of the Federalists, thank you for welcoming me. Lights?
I'm going to speak this evening about our two most important Federalists and the story of their long partnership.
=sigh= to retire, to resign, to give up power willingly is a difficult thing—- I know from recent personal experience.
May, 1796
Your Excellency,
Hamilton, come in my boy!
Remember that in George Washington's time, there were no term limits. His decision to peacefully leave office after two terms — to give up power from a position of strength — was a radical act. And he wanted to mark it with a valedictory for the ages.

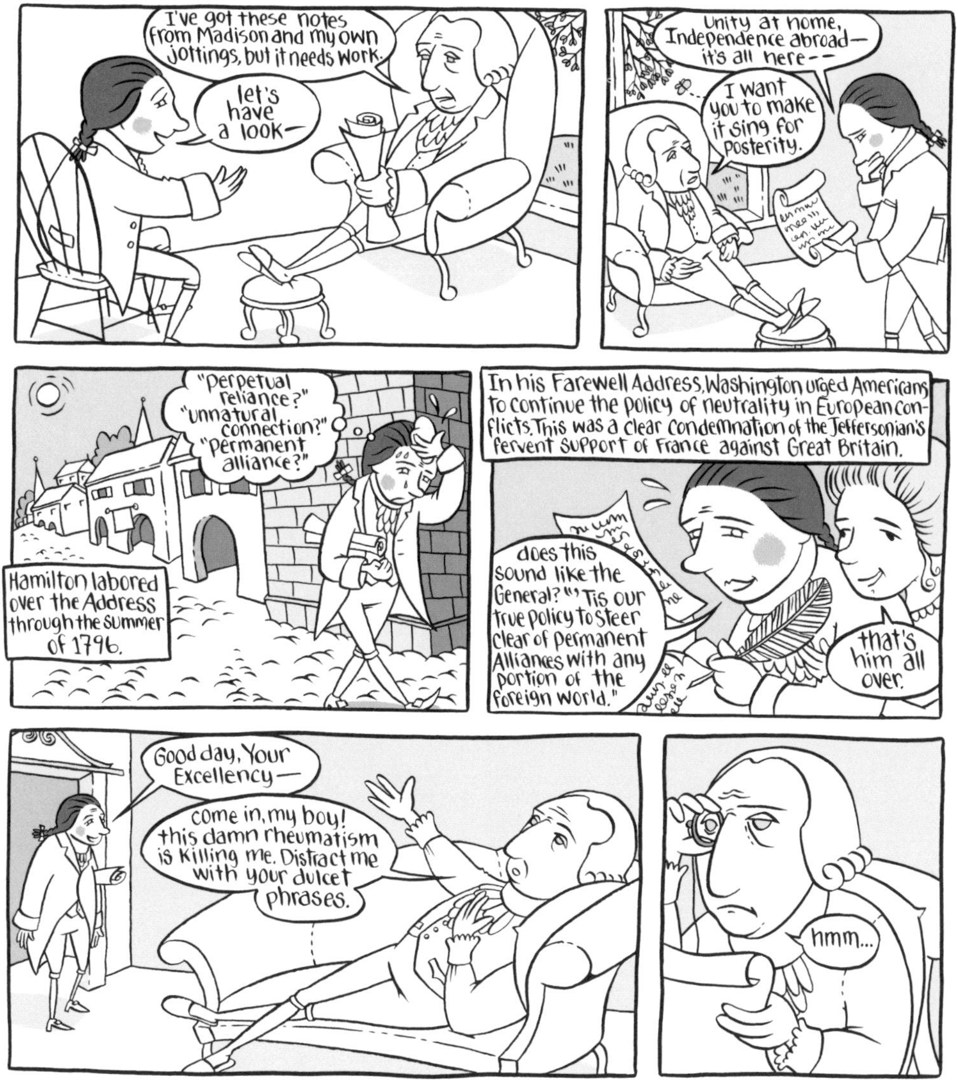
I've got these notes from Madison and my own jottings, but it needs work.
let's have a look—
Unity at home, Independence abroad— it's all here—
I want you to make it sing for posterity.
"perpetual reliance?" "unnatural connection?" "permanent alliance?"
Hamilton labored over the Address through the summer of 1796.
In his Farewell Address, Washington urged Americans to continue the policy of neutrality in European conflicts. This was a clear condemnation of the Jeffersonian's fervent support of France against Great Britain.
does this sound like the General? "'Tis our true policy to steer clear of permanent Alliances with any portion of the foreign world."
that's him all over.
Good day, Your Excellency—
come in, my boy! this damn rheumatism is killing me. Distract me with your dulcet phrases.
hmm...

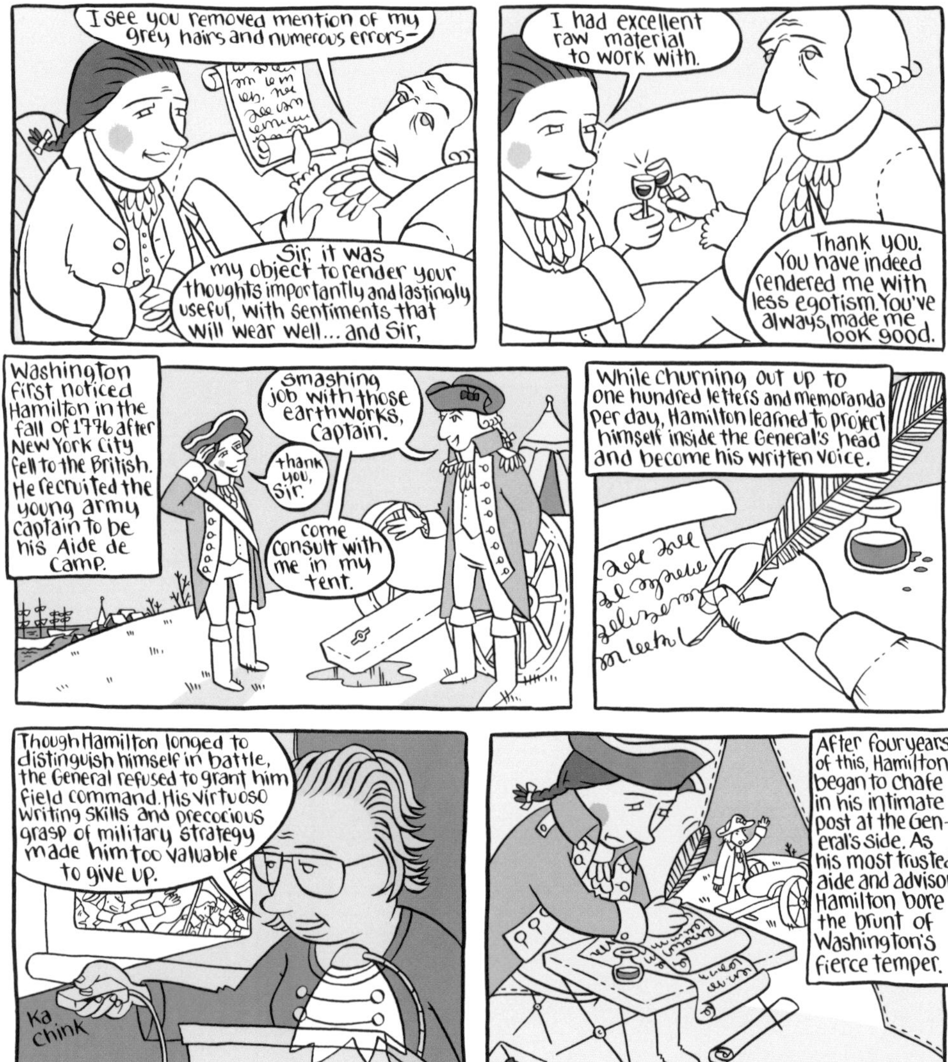
I see you removed mention of my grey hairs and numerous errors–
Sir, it was my object to render your thoughts importantly and lastingly useful, with sentiments that will wear well... and Sir,
I had excellent raw material to work with.
Thank you. You have indeed rendered me with less egotism. You've always made me look good.
Washington first noticed Hamilton in the fall of 1776 after New York City fell to the British. He recruited the young army captain to be his Aide de Camp.
Smashing job with those earthworks, Captain.
thank you, Sir.
Come consult with me in my tent.
While churning out up to one hundred letters and memoranda per day, Hamilton learned to project himself inside the General's head and become his written voice.
Though Hamilton longed to distinguish himself in battle, the General refused to grant him field command. His virtuoso writing skills and precocious grasp of military strategy made him too valuable to give up.
Ka chink
After four years of this, Hamilton began to chafe in his intimate post at the General's side. As his most trusted aide and advisor, Hamilton bore the brunt of Washington's fierce temper.

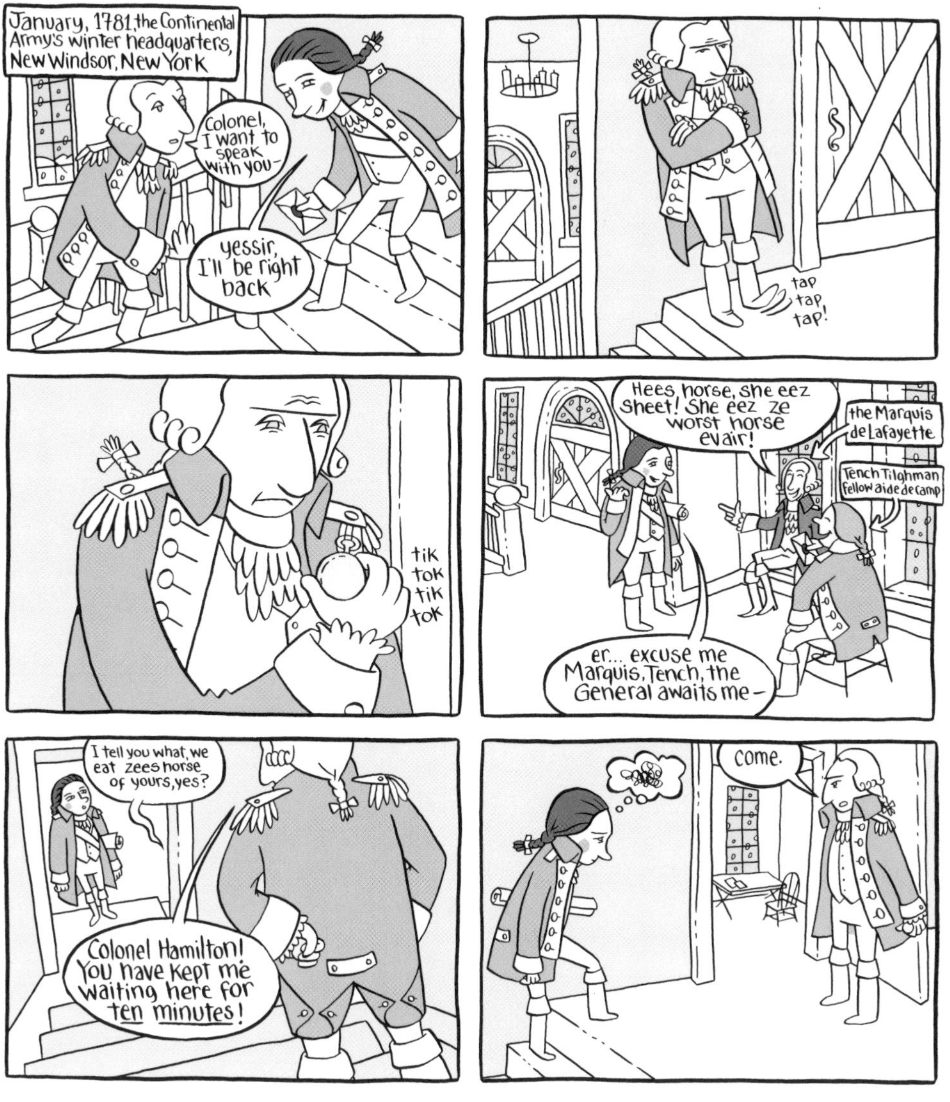
January, 1781, the Continental Army's winter headquarters, New Windsor, New York
Colonel, I want to speak with you—
yessir, I'll be right back
tap tap tap!
tik tok tik tok
Hees horse, she eez sheet! She eez ze worst horse evair!
the Marquis de Lafayette
Tench Tilghman fellow aide de camp
er... excuse me Marquis, Tench, the General awaits me—
I tell you what, we eat zees horse of yours, yes?
Colonel Hamilton! You have kept me waiting here for ten minutes!
come.

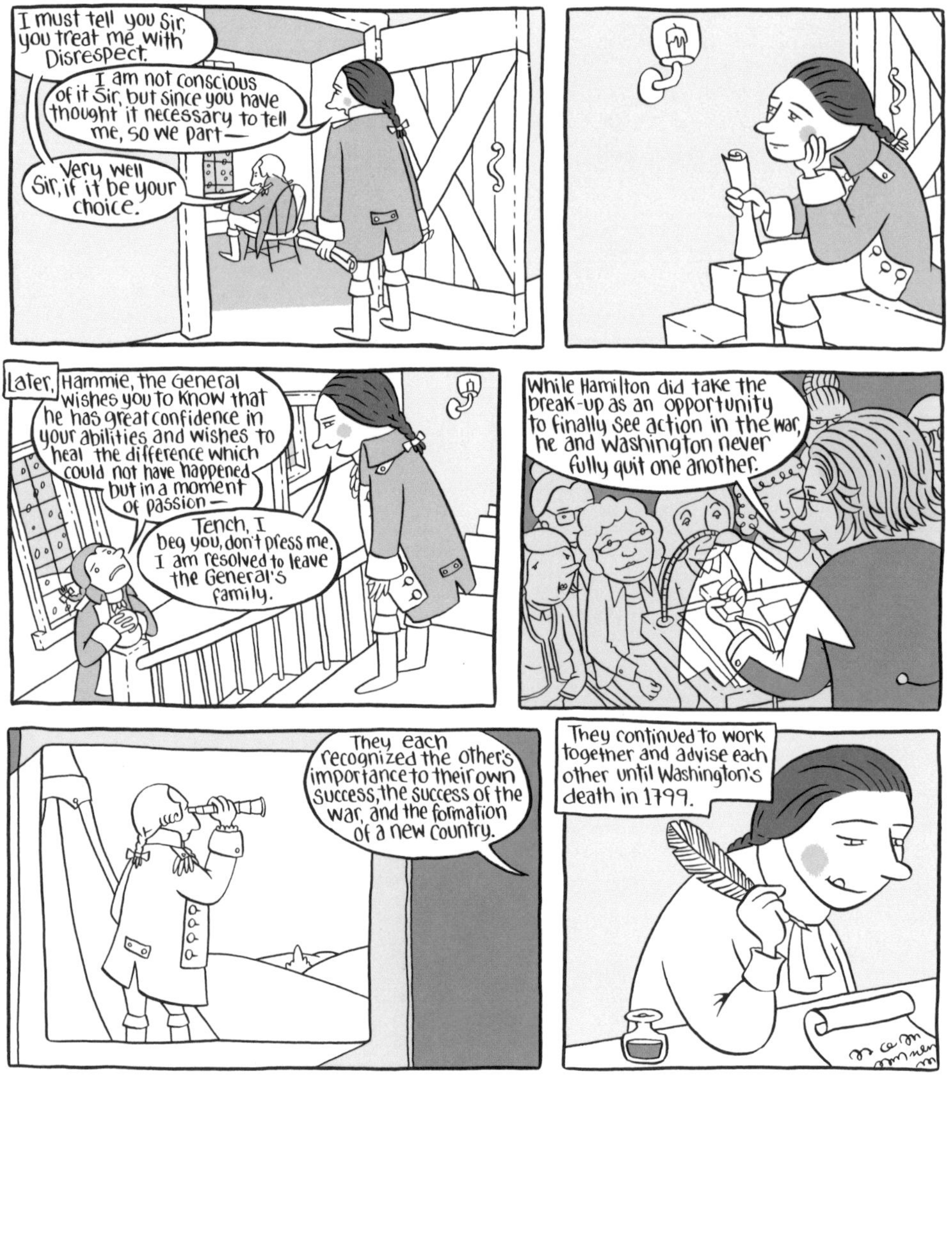
I must tell you Sir, you treat me with Disrespect.
I am not conscious of it Sir, but since you have thought it necessary to tell me, so we part—
Very well Sir, if it be your choice.
Later,
Hammie, the General wishes you to know that he has great confidence in your abilities and wishes to heal the difference which could not have happened but in a moment of passion—
Tench, I beg you, don't press me. I am resolved to leave the General's family.
While Hamilton did take the break-up as an opportunity to finally see action in the war, he and Washington never fully quit one another.
They each recognized the other's importance to their own success, the success of the war, and the formation of a new country.
They continued to work together and advise each other until Washington's death in 1799.

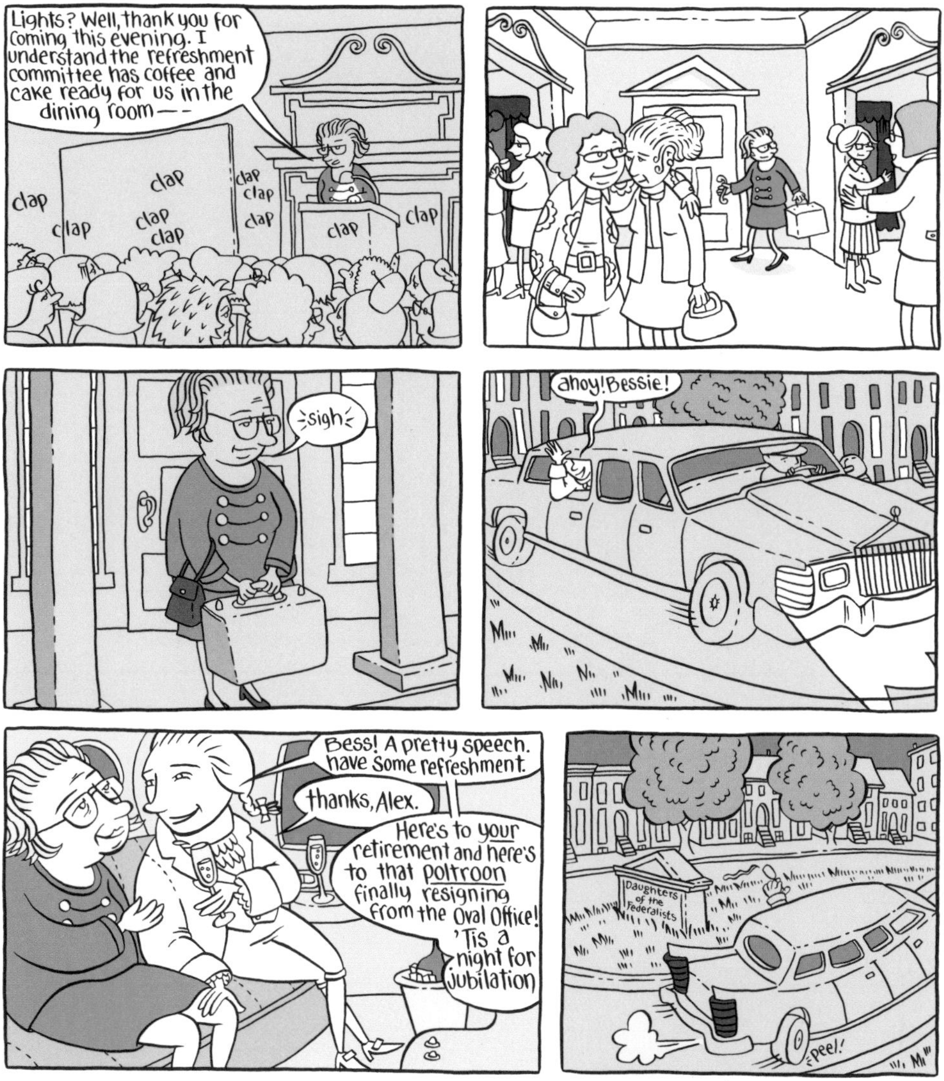

Lights? Well, thank you for coming this evening. I understand the refreshment committee has coffee and cake ready for us in the dining room——
clap
clap
clap
clap
clap
clap
clap
clap
clap
clap
sigh
ahoy! Bessie!
Bess! A pretty speech. have some refreshment.
thanks, Alex.
Here's to your retirement and here's to that poltroon finally resigning from the Oval Office! 'Tis a night for jubilation
Daughters of the Federalists
peel!

by Megan Kelso 1/31/06

Sources: "Alexander Hamilton, American" by Richard Brookhiser.
"Alexander Hamilton" by Ron Chernow.
"Founding Brothers" by Joseph Ellis.
"Alexander Hamilton - Writings" The Library of America, Joanne Freeman, editor.

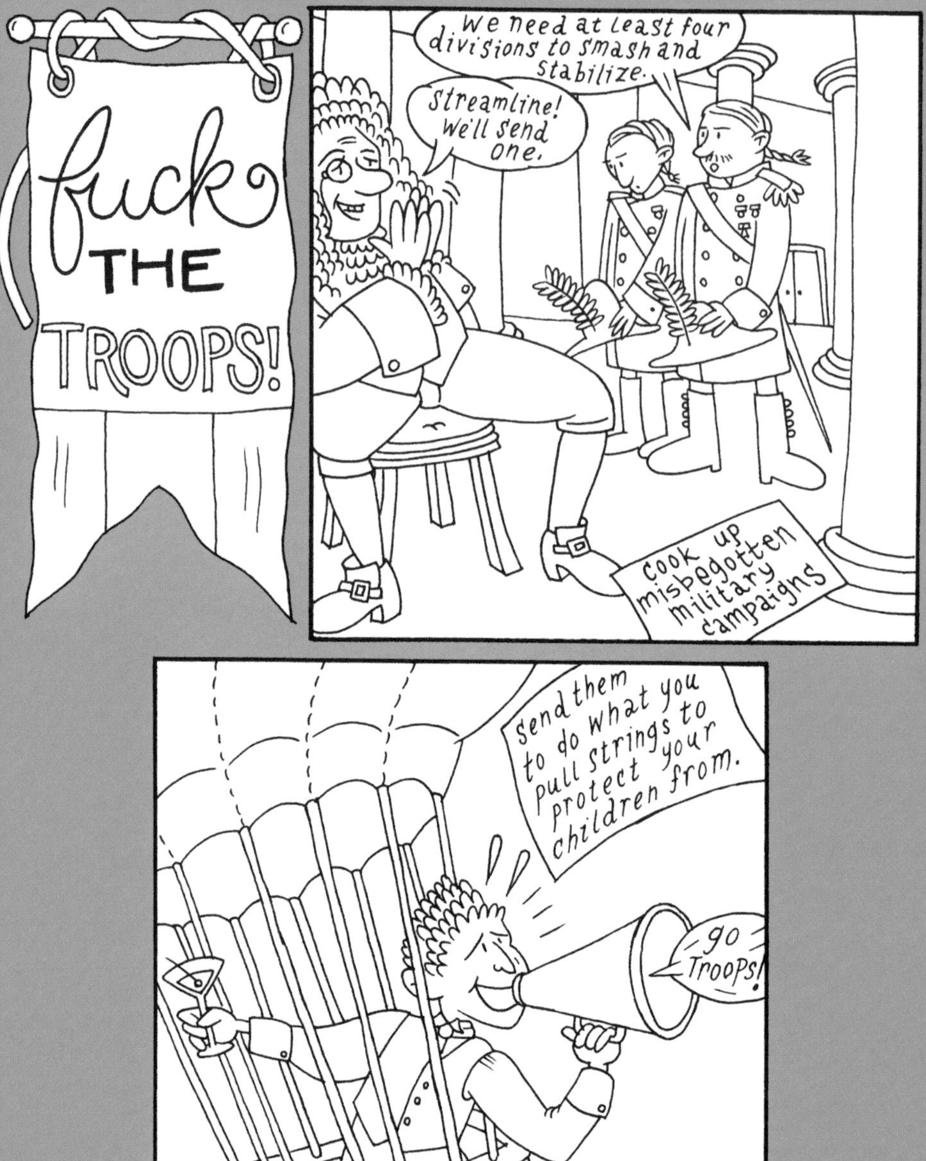
fuck
THE
TROOPS!
We need at least four divisions to smash and stabilize.
Streamline! We'll send one.
cook up misbegotten military campaigns
Send them to do what you pull strings to protect your children from.
go Troops!

non!
nyet!
no!
nein!
fail to get diplomatic support for the war
the enemy are cowards!
downplay the difficulties they'll face in combat
pimp their youth and beauty to the homefront

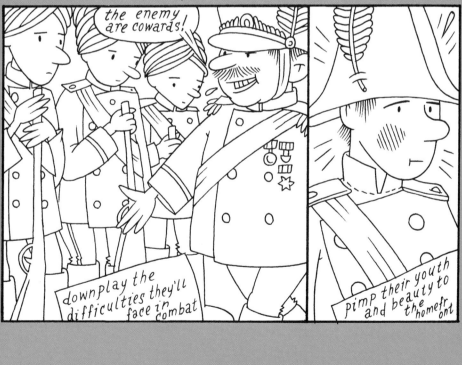

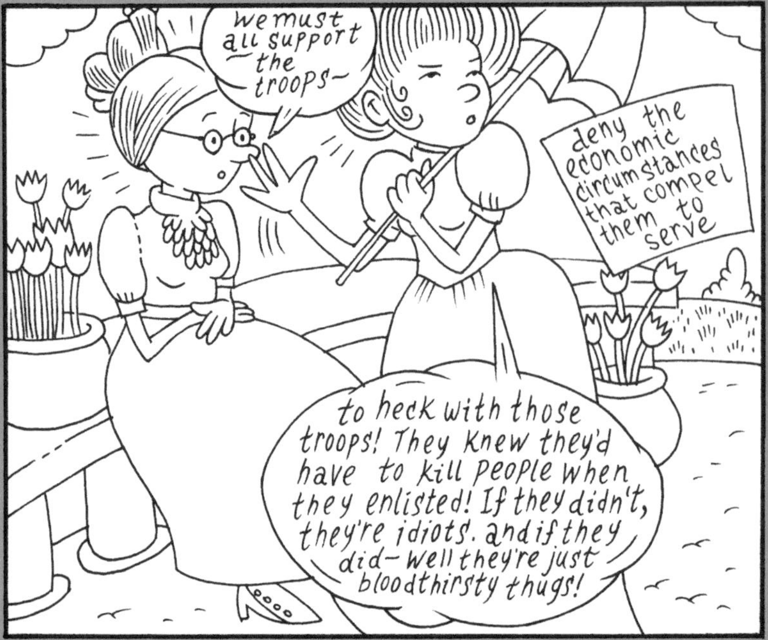
we must all support the troops
deny the economic circumstances that compel them to serve
to heck with those troops! They knew they'd have to kill people when they enlisted! If they didn't, they're idiots. and if they did– well they're just bloodthirsty thugs!

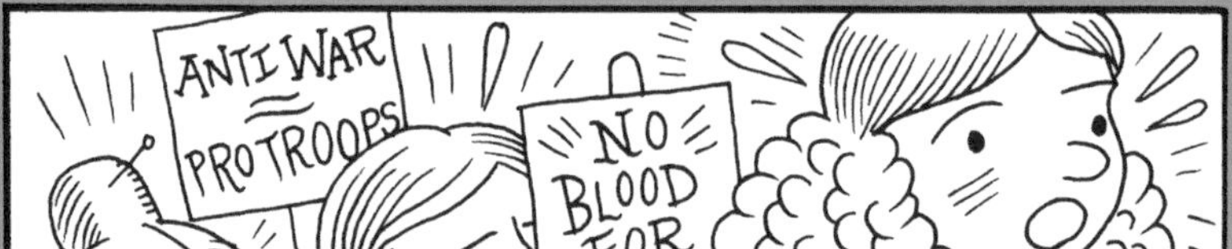
ANTI WAR = PRO TROOPS
NO BLOOD FOR OIL!
NOT IN MY NAME
trivialize their sacrifice with glib sloganeering

train them to kill and revile them for becoming killers.
when troops become vets, forget them.
long after thousands have died and peace has eluded the living, concede that it was all a big mistake.
~©2003~

→ megan kelso & RON REGE, JR.

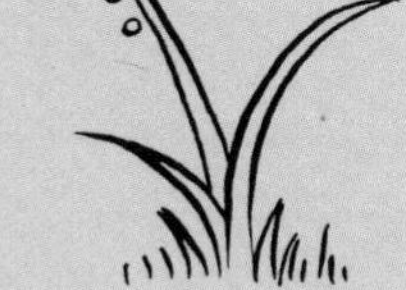

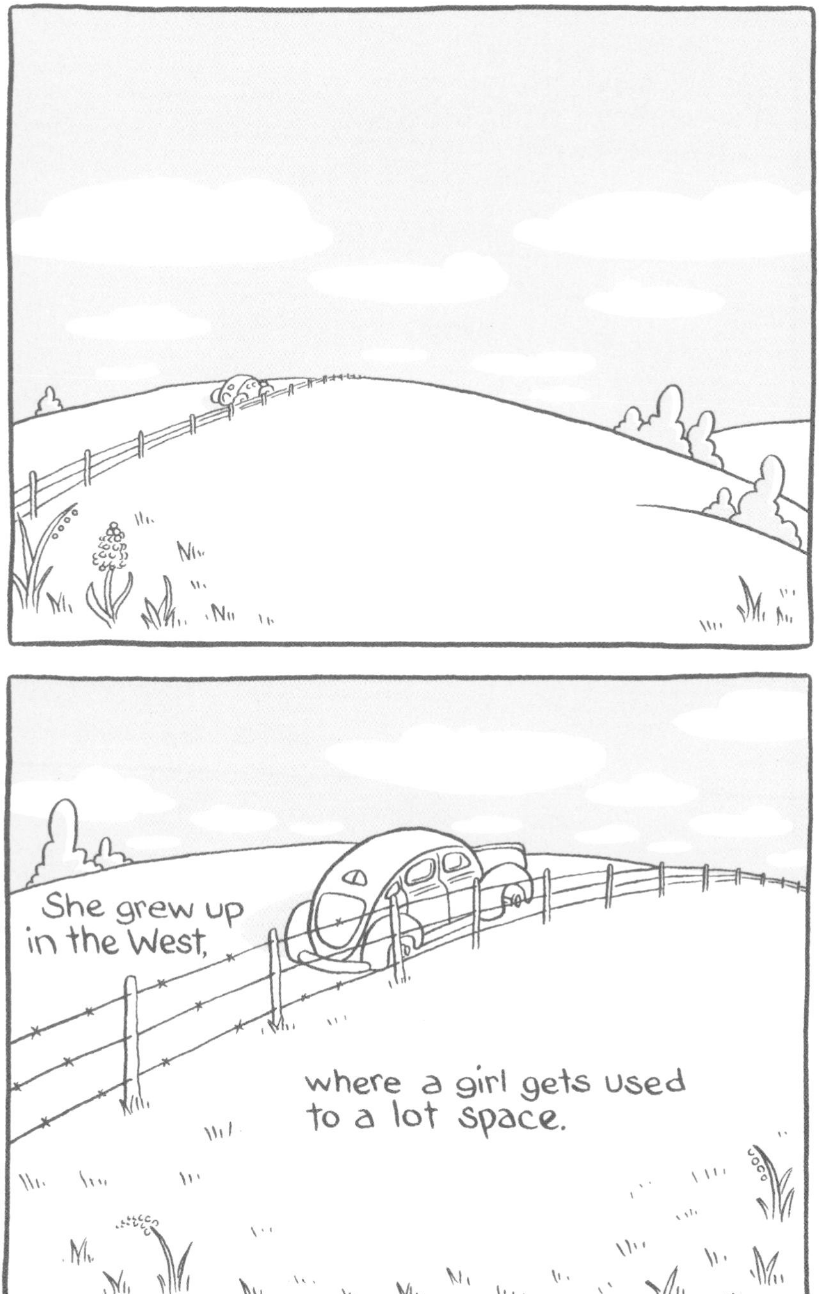
She grew up in the West,
where a girl gets used to a lot space.

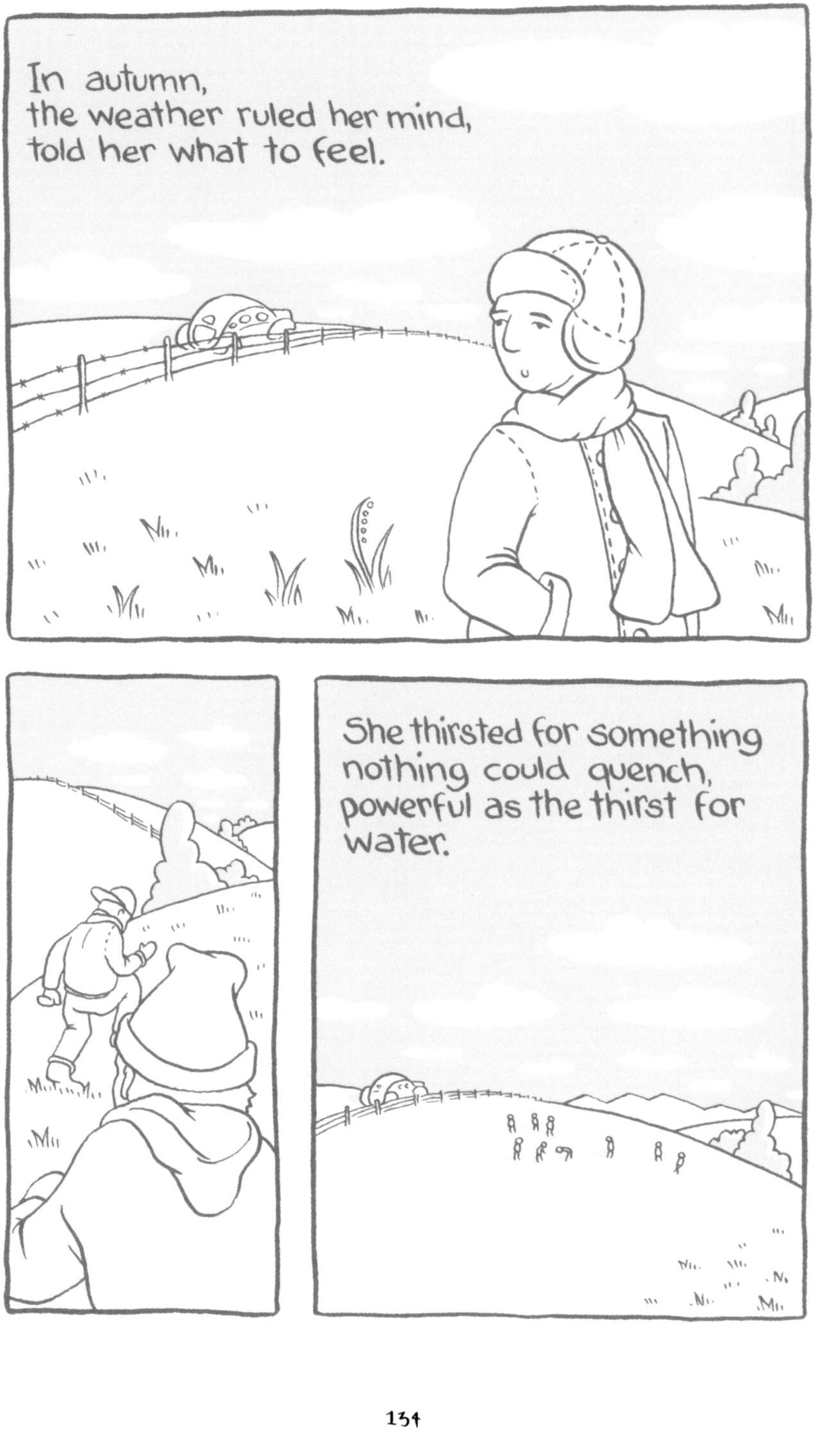
In autumn,
the weather ruled her mind,
told her what to feel.
She thirsted for something
nothing could quench,
powerful as the thirst for
water.

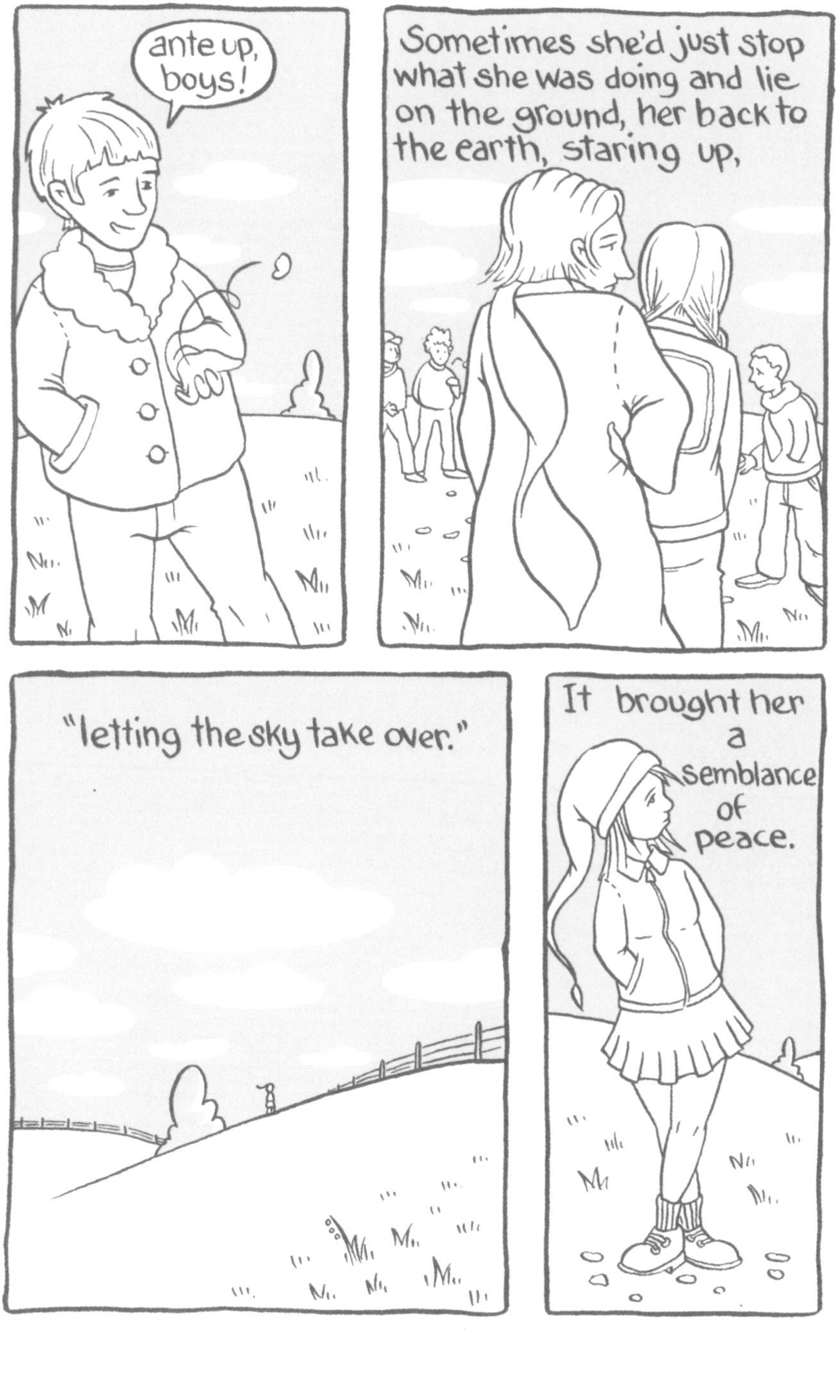
ante up, boys!
Sometimes she'd just stop what she was doing and lie on the ground, her back to the earth, staring up,
"letting the sky take over."
It brought her a semblance of peace.

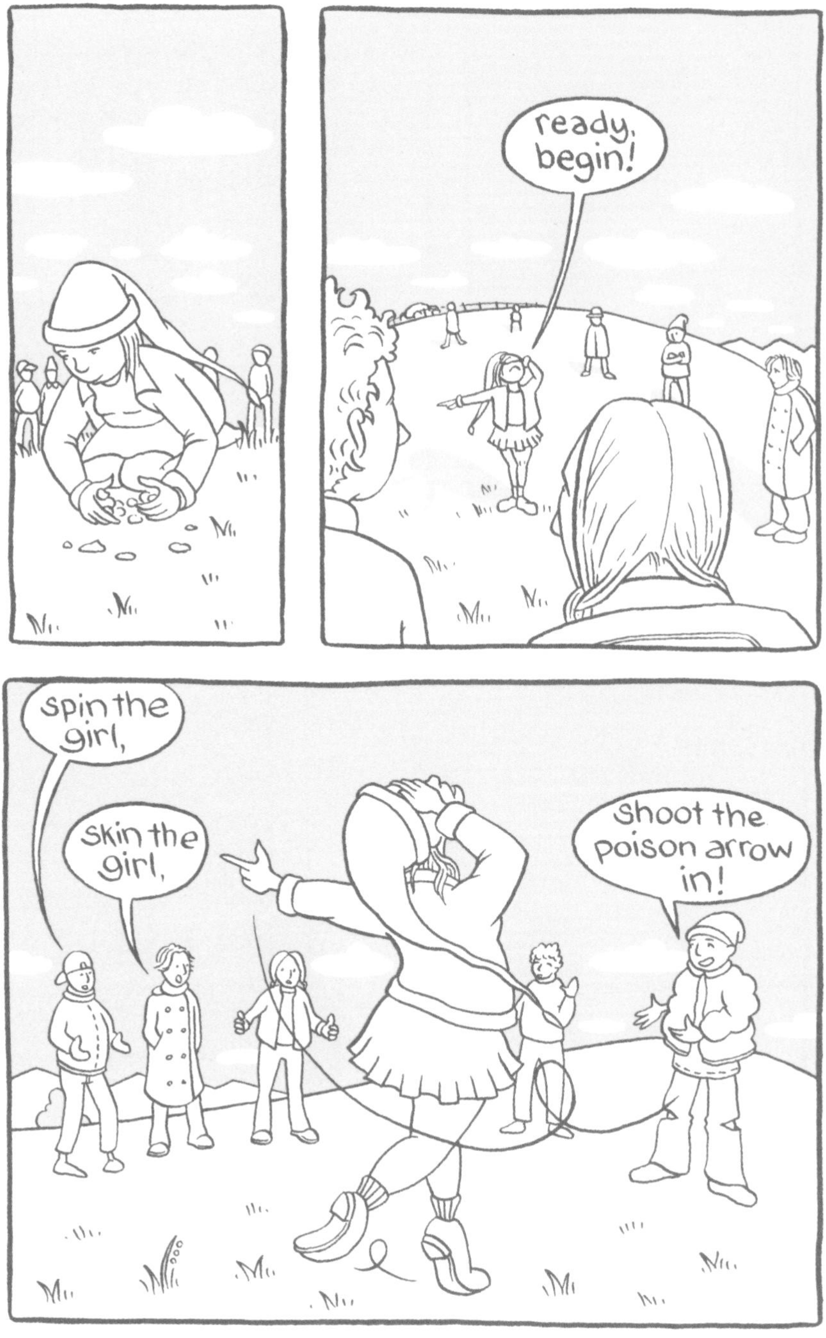
ready, begin!
spin the girl,
skin the girl,
shoot the poison arrow in!

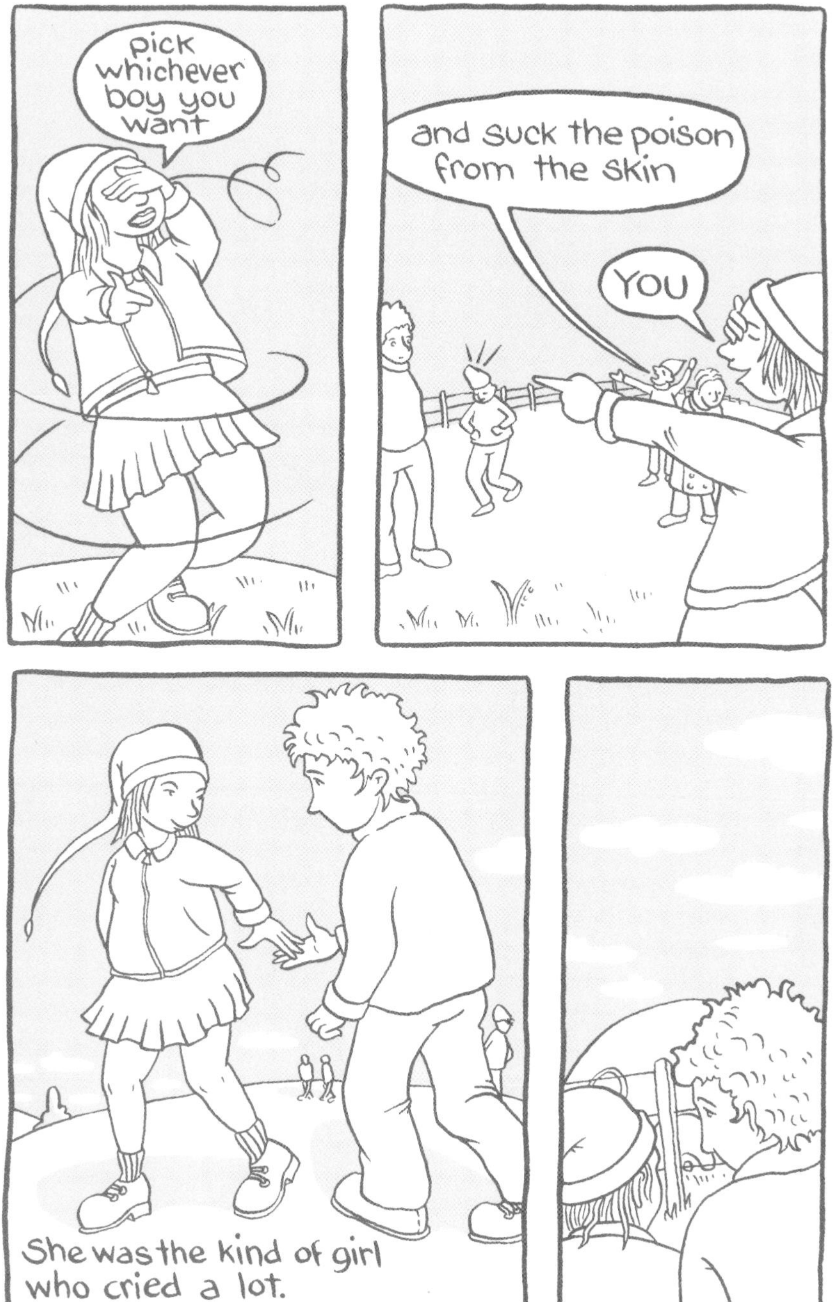
pick whichever boy you want
and suck the poison from the skin
YOU
She was the kind of girl who cried a lot.

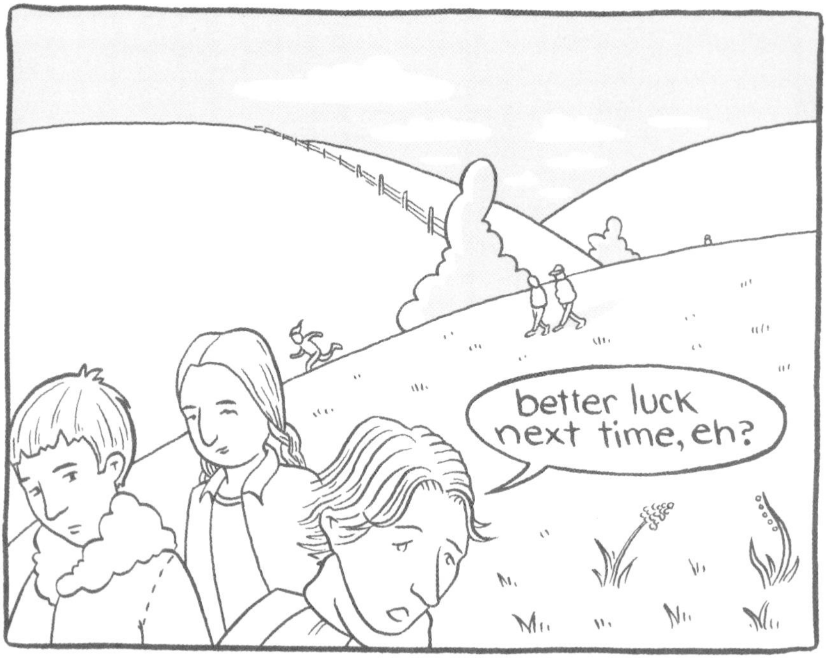
better luck next time, eh?

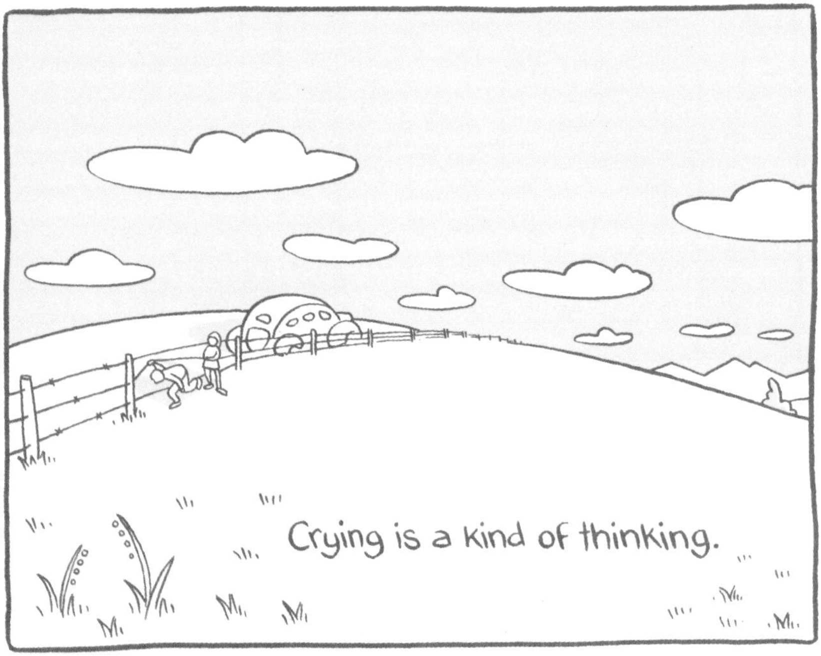
Crying is a kind of thinking.

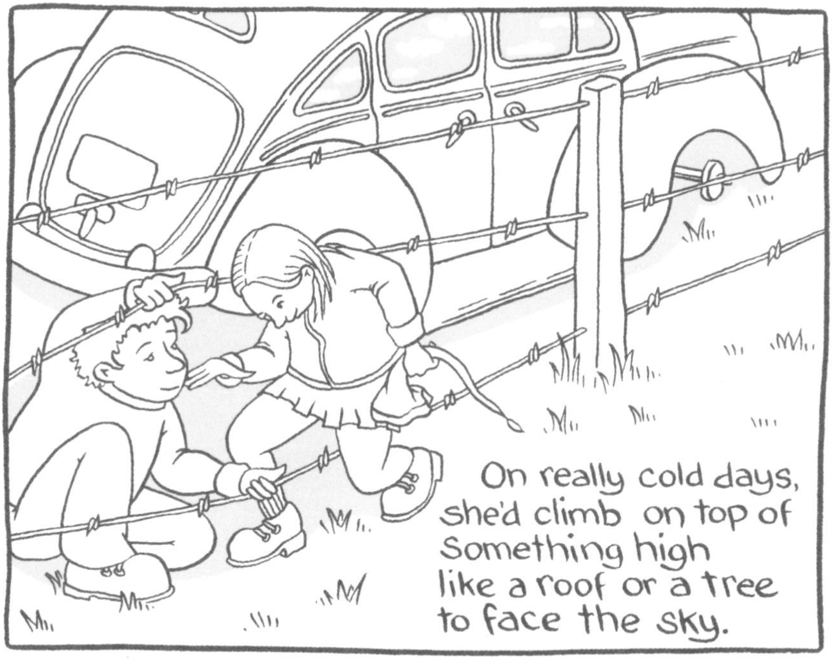
On really cold days,
she'd climb on top of
something high
like a roof or a tree
to face the sky.

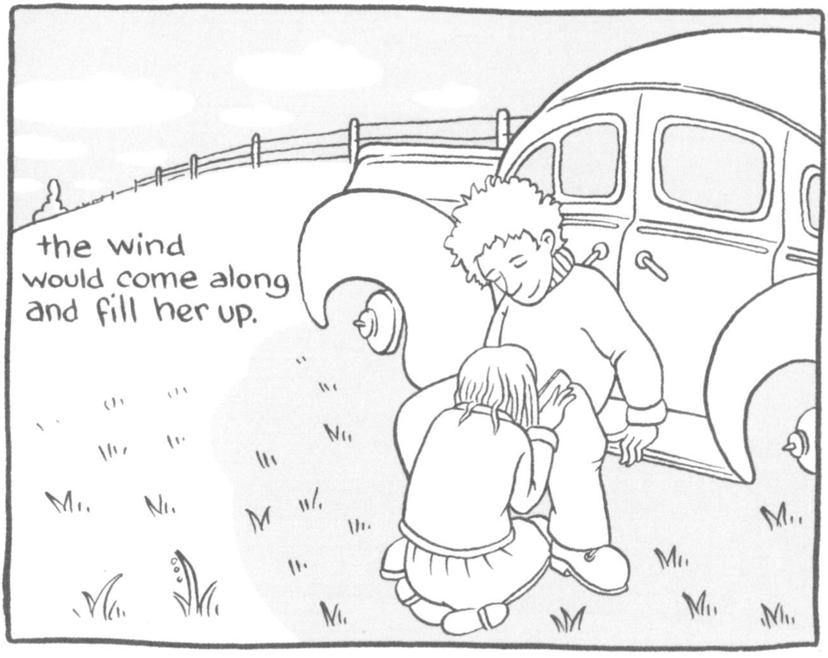
the wind
would come along
and fill her up.

She did these things to stay alive.

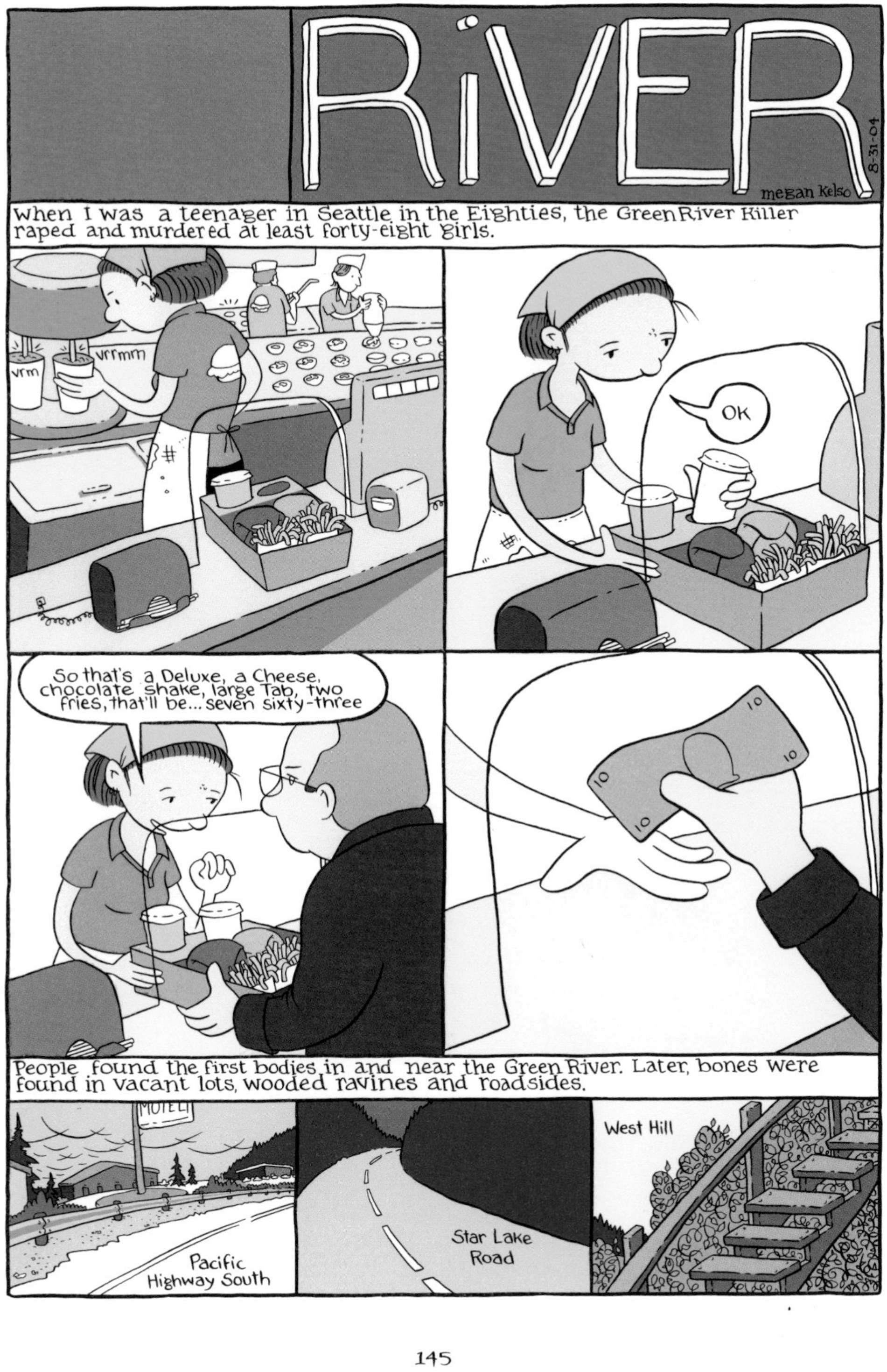
RiVER
8-31-04
megan Kelso
When I was a teenager in Seattle in the Eighties, the Green River Killer raped and murdered at least forty-eight girls.
vrm
vrrmm
OK
So that's a Deluxe, a Cheese, chocolate shake, large Tab, two fries, that'll be... seven sixty-three
10
10
10
10
People found the first bodies in and near the Green River. Later, bones were found in vacant lots, wooded ravines and roadsides.
MOTEL
Pacific Highway South
Star Lake Road
West Hill

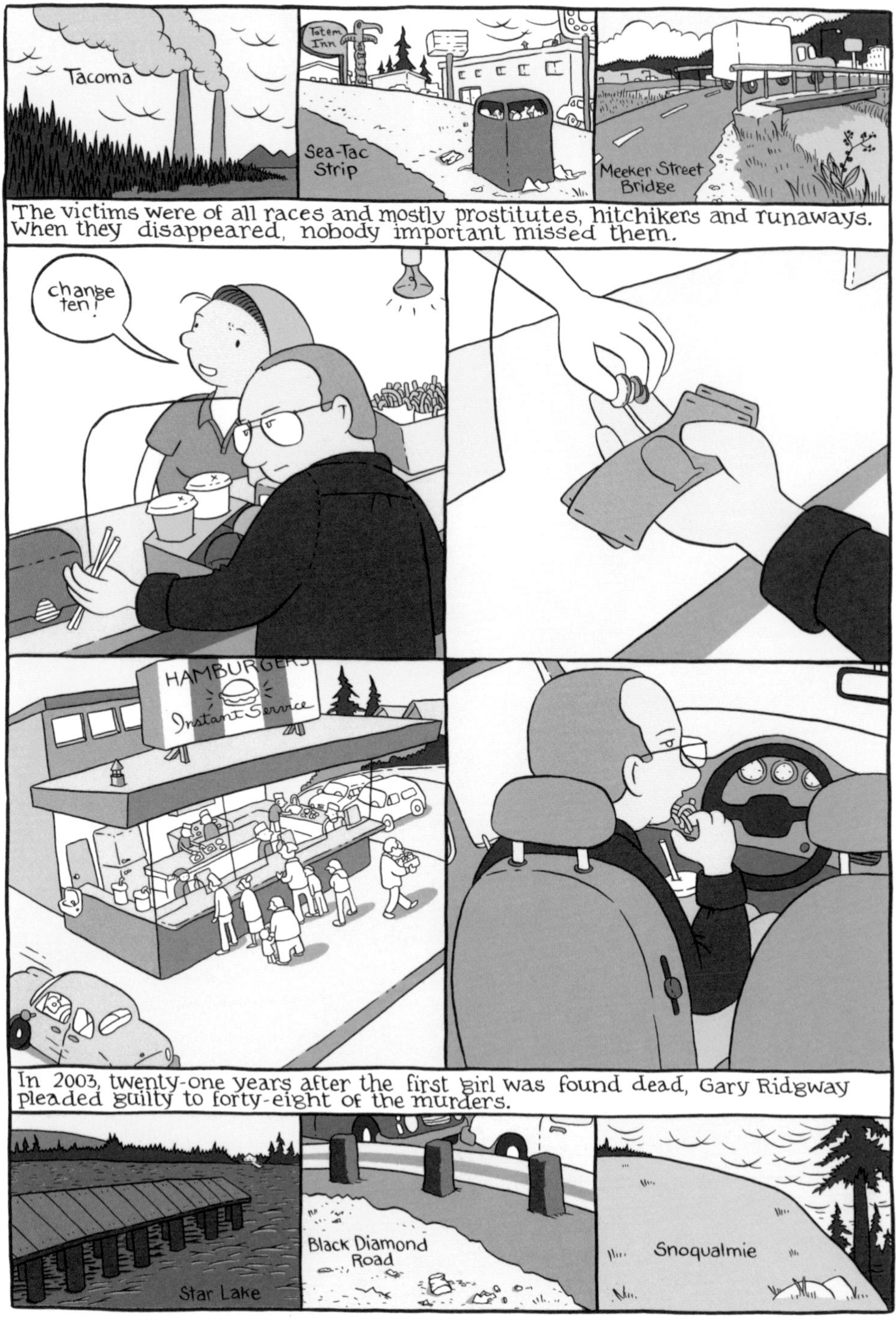
Tacoma
Totem Inn
Sea-Tac Strip
Meeker Street Bridge
The victims were of all races and mostly prostitutes, hitchikers and runaways. When they disappeared, nobody important missed them.
change ten!
HAMBURGERS
Instant Service
In 2003, twenty-one years after the first girl was found dead, Gary Ridgway pleaded guilty to forty-eight of the murders.
Star Lake
Black Diamond Road
Snoqualmie

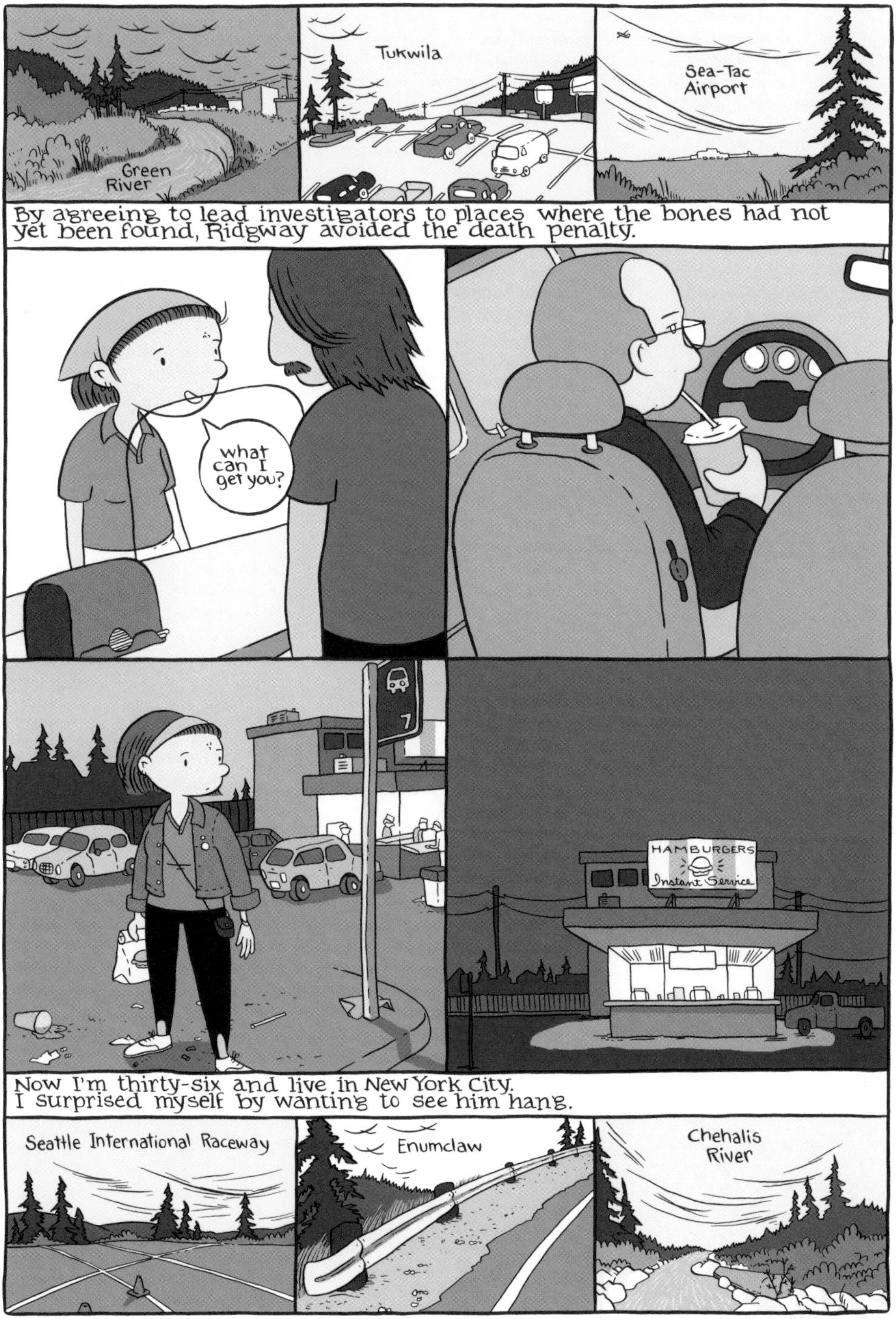
Green River
Tukwila
Sea-Tac Airport
By agreeing to lead investigators to places where the bones had not yet been found, Ridgway avoided the death penalty.
what can I get you?
HAMBURGERS
Instant Service
Now I'm thirty-six and live in New York City.
I surprised myself by wanting to see him hang.
Seattle International Raceway
Enumclaw
Chehalis River